THE DARK AGES

Colin and Sarah McEvedy

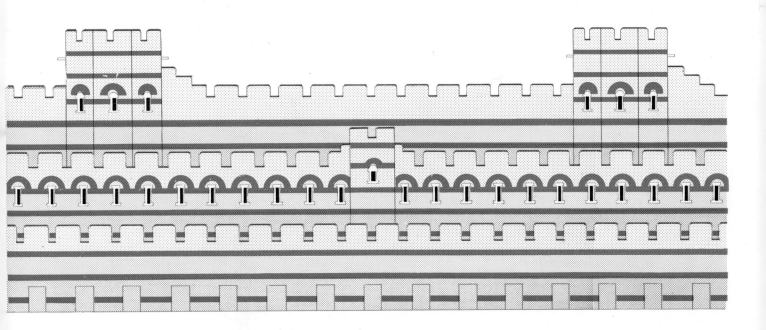

A Crowell-Collier Press Book
THE MACMILLAN COMPANY
New York, New York

COVER

The prow of the Viking ship from the Oseberg burial
mound in Vestfold, Norway.

The Viking nobility liked to take their ships with them
when they died. Sometimes the ship was used as a funeral
pyre, sometimes it was buried and the site covered with a
mound of earth. The Oseberg mound, excavated in 1904,
is an exceptionally fine example of a ship burial. It
contained the body of a young woman but though she was
obviously someone important no one knows exactly who
she was. She took a lot more than her boat on her last
journey: in the burial chamber was everything needed to
furnish an aristocrat's household. In and around it lay the
bodies of an old servant woman, four dogs, an ox and
fifteen horses.

The ship itself is only a little smaller than the Gokstad
ship described on p. 39. But it is nothing like as strongly
built nor is it high enough to cope with heavy seas. So it
was probably only used for coastal journeys such as a
princess might make in fair weather. Where it scores over
the Gokstad ship is in its carving. This is rich, intricate
and almost perfectly preserved. Both stem and stern posts
end in similar spirals: the stem spiral contains a miniature
dragon's head. The stern, which is incomplete, presumably
had the dragon's tail.

TITLE PAGE

Part of the Theodosian walls of Constantinople. They
cover the 7 km between Blachernae and the Sea of
Marmora. The rear wall was built in 413, the wall in
front was added in 447. The third wall is only a parapet
on the edge of the dry moat that runs in front of the
whole system.

The walls are built of concrete faced with limestone
blocks. Every 3 m there is a band of brickwork which
runs the width of the wall and binds it together. The
towers are not bonded into the wall – a tower weighs
more than an equal length of wall and is likely to settle
further and faster. Building them separately allows them
to settle at their own rates.

The big towers, of which there are 96 in all, average
18 m in height. Most of them are square. Others have
six, seven or, as here, eight sides. The 10 m towers on
the second wall are alternately square and crescent shaped.

Library of Congress Catalog Card Number 72–178600

The Macmillan Company
866 Third Avenue
New York, New York 10022

Printed in Great Britain

Contents

The maps are all drawn with north at the top except the map of Constantinople on p. 14 and the map of Samarra on p. 58
All dates are AD unless BC is specified.

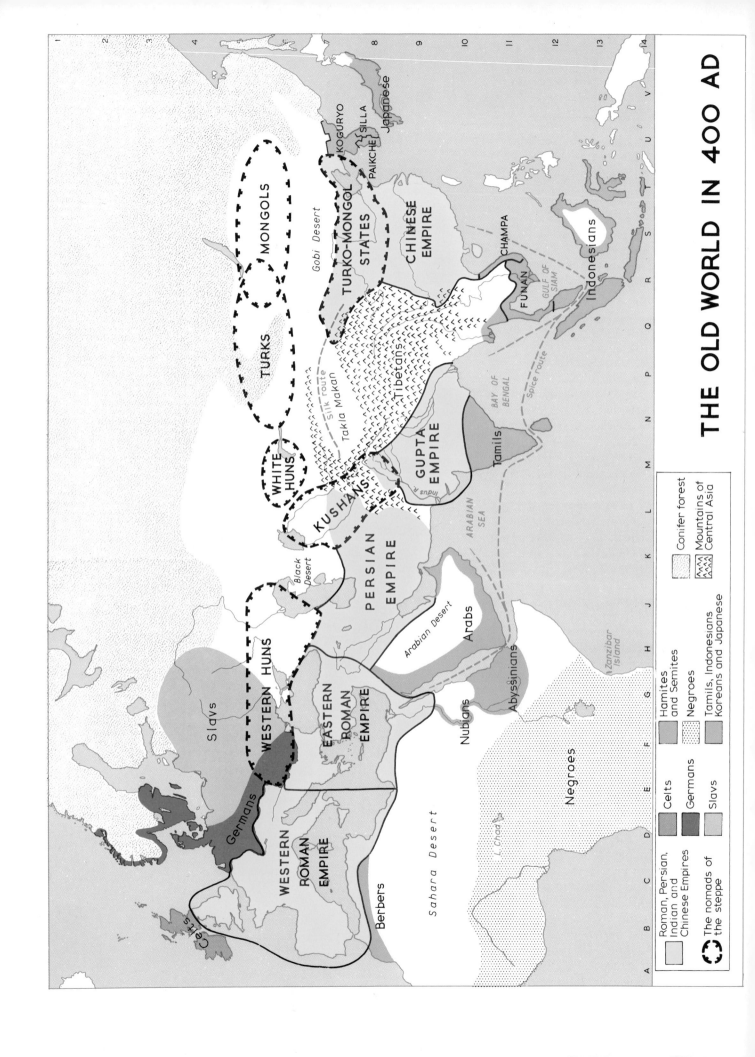

THE OLD WORLD IN 400 AD

Legend:
- Roman, Persian, Indian and Chinese Empires
- The nomads of the steppe
- Celts
- Germans
- Slavs
- Hamites and Semites
- Negroes
- Tamils, Indonesians Koreans and Japanese
- Conifer forest
- Mountains of Central Asia

Labels on map:

WESTERN ROMAN EMPIRE
EASTERN ROMAN EMPIRE
PERSIAN EMPIRE
GUPTA EMPIRE
CHINESE EMPIRE
KUSHANS
WESTERN HUNS
WHITE HUNS
TURKS
MONGOLS
TURKO-MONGOL STATES
Germans
Slavs
Celts
Berbers
Nubians
Abyssinians
Arabs
Negroes
Tamils
Indonesians
Tibetans
KOGURYO
SILLA
PAIKCHE
Japanese
CHAMPA
FUNAN

Geographic features:
Sahara Desert
Arabian Desert
Black Desert
Gobi Desert
Takla Makan
ARABIAN SEA
BAY OF BENGAL
GULF OF SIAM
L. Chad
Zanzibar Island
Indus R.
Silk route
Spice route

The Four Empires and the Nomads of the Steppe
400

1 Arcadius, East Roman emperor 395–408, with members of his bodyguard

2 Horse-archer from the Manchurian steppe

In the 4th century AD the world held something over 200 million people. Most of them – about 160 million – were crowded into the belt of farming land that runs across the Old World from Europe via Persia and India to China. And in this agricultural zone lay the world's only literate, organized states.

There were four of these – the Roman, Persian, Indian and Chinese Empires. Each was the result of a long process in which smaller states had swallowed each other up until finally the winner had come up against some natural limit – usually the mountains or deserts that marked the edges of the agricultural zone. So each was a near-complete segment of the farming belt.

These empires were not only large, they were also long-lived. The Gupta Empire was new, only 50 years old in 400 AD, but the Roman and Chinese Empires had been in existence for 600 years and the Persian (in one form or another) for 1000.

The political scene in 400 had its complications. There were nomads in north China (of which more below) and the Roman Empire had been divided between Honorius and Arcadius, the two sons of the emperor Theodosius. But men still thought of the civilized world in terms of the traditional empires and confidently expected that one day the old boundaries would be restored.

The nomads occupied the steppe zone of Europe and Asia – the rolling grasslands that stretch from south Russia to Manchuria. They were illiterate herdsmen constantly on the move (that is what nomad means) as they looked for pasture for their flocks. There were very few nomads, probably only three or four million. This may seem too few for them to have presented any threat to the great empires, but in war numbers are not the only factor. At this time cavalry was the decisive arm. The nomad lived in the saddle: nomad armies might be small but they were all cavalry, and this made them formidable.

There were three main races on the steppe: the Huns, the Turks and the Mongols. Each consisted of many tribes and the tribes were constantly crossing each other's paths. So though it is true that the Huns dominated the western end of the steppe, the Turks the centre and the Mongols Mongolia, there were tribes of each in each area. It was a Hun chieftain, for example, who set up the first nomad-ruled state in North China.

China had nomads all along its northern frontier and by 400 it had lost half its territory to nomad invaders. The other empires were luckier because they were not in direct contact with the steppe. The Indians were protected by the mountains of central Asia. The Persians had a buffer state in the Kushan kingdom.[1] The Romans also had a buffer on their frontier: the German peasantry. When the western Huns moved into Europe it was the Germans who suffered first. Many of them had to take refuge in the empire they had previously been fighting.

The great empires made up the civilized world. Their cities contained the schools, the craftsmen and the administrators necessary to keep a complex society functioning. Their libraries contained the accumulated experience of mankind. If they fell to the assaults of the barbarians, civilization itself would be in peril.

And by 400 both Rome and China were fighting for their lives.

TRADE ROUTES

The Near East and the Far East were connected by two trade routes. The first ran overland north of the mountains of central Asia. The Romans called this the Silk Route – silk was their main import from China. The journey from the Chinese frontier to Persia took about six months.

The second route was by sea along the southern rim of Asia. This was called the Spice Route because pepper from India and spices from Indonesia were the main goods coming to Rome this way. The sea captains who sailed the Spice Route used the monsoon winds to cut across the Arabian Sea, the Bay of Bengal and the Gulf of Siam. Each of these hops took about a month. But because the monsoon blows for a short season, usually only a single hop was made in a year. What with waiting for connections – Roman ships never went further east than Ceylon, nor Indonesian ships further west than south India – it would have been a lucky traveller who got from Rome to China in two years by sea.

A cross route connected the Silk and Spice Routes via the Kushan kingdom and the Indus River. It was also possible to get from China to the Bay of Bengal via Burma.

None of these routes carried much traffic – a dozen or so ships or a caravan or two a year. Rome and China remained barely aware of each other's existence, and half of what they thought they knew was nonsense about monsters guarding caves full of gold. Each considered itself the centre of the world and the only really civilized state.

[1] The Kushans were nomads who had been driven off the steppe by the Huns and now ran a half-nomad, half-farming state that extended from Turkestan via Afghanistan to northwest India.

5

The Turkish Empire of North China 400-550

3 Northern Wei cavalryman

Between the Gobi desert and the agricultural land of China there is a belt of grassland or steppe country. This is known as Inner Mongolia because from the Chinese point of view it is on the inner side of the Gobi. Outer Mongolia – the present-day state of Mongolia – is the steppe on the far side of the Gobi.

The Chinese had more trouble with their Inner Mongolian frontier than with all their other frontiers put together. The nomads who lived in the area were dangerous enemies and unreliable allies. The Great Wall was built in an attempt to solve this problem but was not in itself enough. Through most of Chinese history the bulk of the army had to be stationed near the Wall.

Because nomads made superb cavalry the Chinese were always eager to have them in their army. Very often the authorities hired more than was sensible and the nomad cavalry regiments could then hold the empire to ransom. It was difficult to know what to do. Leaving the nomads outside the empire meant they were always attacking the frontier provinces: bringing them in meant a constant risk of rebellion.

Throughout the 4th century China was seriously harassed by nomads. As early as 308 one nomad chieftain, a Hun commanding the garrison of the frontier town of T'ai-yuan, had declared himself emperor of China. Soon his son had taken Loyang and Ch'ang-an, the two imperial capitals, and conquered most of the Yellow River valley. The real Chinese emperor was forced to flee to the Yangtze where he ruled what was left of his empire from Nanking ('south capital'). The Chinese state was split in two.

The dynasty founded by the Huns in the north did not stay in power for long. Other chieftains set themselves up as rival emperors; new dynasties came and went every few years until the end of the century. Then in 398 the Turkish governor of P'ing-ch'eng started to put together a more lasting structure. By the 430s the dynasty he founded (the Chinese call it the Northern Wei dynasty) had brought the whole of the Yellow River valley under its control.[1]

This Turkish Empire of north China was a vigorous state. It pressed hard on the Chinese Empire of the Yangtze valley. Its armies also patrolled the caravan stations of the Silk Route as far west as the Takla Makan and, when necessary, crossed the Gobi to punish the Jouan-jouan Mongols for raiding.

4 Since the 1st century AD Indian missionaries had been bringing Buddhism to China – overland along the Silk Route, by sea via the Spice Route. During the 5th century the missionary effort paid off: China became a Buddhist country. Within a generation there were monasteries in every town and Buddhist monks numbered tens of thousands.

Little remains of all this today. The Chinese built in wood and the monasteries that were not burnt down have long since decayed away. However there are some impressive rock-cut shrines. This one is part of a series at Yun-kang a few kilometres west of the original Northern Wei capital, P'ing-ch'eng. The figure of the Buddha on the left is 13.7 m high.

[1] The Chinese call the confused 90-year period between the first Hun rebellion of 308 and the final Turkish rising of 398 'the period of the sixteen states' but there were really only four power bases competing for control.

As shown on map B the four are: 1. The Huns of T'ai-yuan (known to Chinese history as the Chao dynasty). 2. The Mongols of Liao-tung (the Yen dynasty). 3. The Tibetan mercenaries who held the western capital, Ch'ang-an (the Ch'in dynasty). 4. The Huns of Hsia (the Hsia dynasty). The Chinese sub-divide most of these to get a total of eleven dynasties and they count as five more the various Liang dynasties that rose and fell in the backwater province of Kansu.

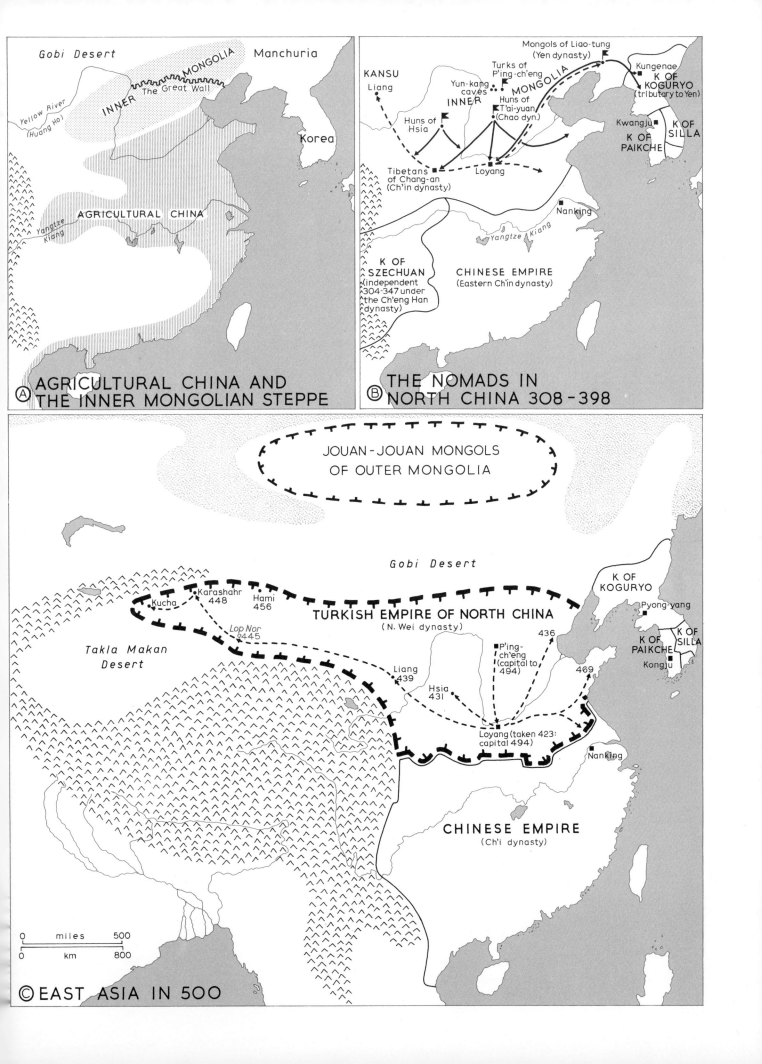

A AGRICULTURAL CHINA AND THE INNER MONGOLIAN STEPPE

Gobi Desert
INNER MONGOLIA
The Great Wall
Manchuria
Yellow River (Huang Ho)
Korea
AGRICULTURAL CHINA
Yangtze Kiang

B THE NOMADS IN NORTH CHINA 308-398

Mongols of Liao-tung (Yen dynasty)
KANSU
Liang
Turks of P'ing-ch'eng
Yun-kang caves
INNER MONGOLIA
Huns of T'ai-yuan (Chao dyn.)
Kungenae
K OF KOGURYO (tributary to Yen)
Huns of Hsia
Kwangju
K OF PAIKCHE
K OF SILLA
Tibetans of Chang-an (Ch'in dynasty)
Loyang
Nanking
Yangtze Kiang
K OF SZECHUAN (independent 304-347 under the Ch'eng Han dynasty)
CHINESE EMPIRE (Eastern Ch'in dynasty)

C EAST ASIA IN 500

JOUAN-JOUAN MONGOLS OF OUTER MONGOLIA

Gobi Desert
K OF KOGURYO
Pyong-yang
Kucha
Karashahr 448
Hami 456
TURKISH EMPIRE OF NORTH CHINA (N. Wei dynasty)
436
Lop Nor ?445
P'ing-ch'eng (capital to 494)
K OF SILLA
K OF PAIKCHE
Kongju
Takla Makan Desert
Liang 439
Hsia 431
469
Loyang (taken 423: capital 494)
Nanking
CHINESE EMPIRE (Ch'i dynasty)

miles 0 — 500
km 0 — 800

Huns, Germans and the Fall of Rome 380-453

5 Stilicho, commander of the army of the West Roman Empire 394–408

Something had gone very wrong with the Roman Empire by AD 380.

It is not easy to be sure what it was because Roman historians wrote about emperors and battles, not about economics. But it seems likely that the army was costing more than the empire could afford. Certainly taxes had got so high that the small farmers who made up 90 per cent of the empire's population stopped coming to the market towns where the taxes were paid. In consequence the towns dwindled away and the government's revenue fell catastrophically. The army had been asking for more money: suddenly there was no money at all.

This dismal view of the empire is only really true of the western half. The eastern half had a population that was more concentrated and easier to administer and tax. In particular it had Egypt, the most profitable province of all. In a real crisis the East could always raise money from somewhere. When the empire came under attack blows fell on both East and West but it was the West that collapsed.

The barbarians on the empire's frontier in Europe were the Germans. Too weak to break into the empire in the first two centuries AD, they had spread out from Germany to the Black Sea as they multiplied. By 380 they were strong enough to break in but too divided, and too poorly led, to succeed.

The most powerful tribes were two groups of Goths – the Visigoths (West Goths) and Ostrogoths (East Goths). Living as they did on the steppe along the north shore of the Black Sea where horsemanship was a tradition, the Goths built up a strong cavalry. This made them much more formidable than the other German tribes who could only field armies of foot soldiers. But although Gothic cavalry was good, the cavalry of the steppe people was better. In 372 the Ostrogothic king Ermanarich was foolish enough to attack the Huns who lived beyond the Don. His disastrous defeat and the Hun invasion that followed sent both tribes of Goths spinning westward into the Roman Empire.

The Roman administrators did their best to settle the defeated Goths in the Balkans but the Goths made poor civilians. They thought of themselves as warriors and their idea of a hero was a robber-king. They constantly broke out on plundering expeditions.

At this time Arcadius, emperor of the Eastern Roman Empire, and Honorius, emperor of the western half, were not getting on as well as brothers might. In particular they were quarrelling about Illyria (modern Yugoslavia). Arcadius saw a way of turning his Gothic problem into an asset: he suggested to the Visigoths that they occupy Illyria on his behalf (401). Soon the Visigoths were facing the army of the West on the frontier of Italy.

The general in command of the Western Empire's army was Stilicho.[1] He called in all available troops from the Rhine frontier and from Britain and paid them by stripping gold from the temples of Rome. In 402 and again in 408 he defeated the Visigoths. He also annihilated a force of Suevi and Ostrogoths that invaded Italy in 406.

But the price was high. The Vandals and Suevi swarmed across the undefended Rhine into France and Spain and half the Western Empire disappeared. The rest of it followed soon after when Honorius grew frightened of Stilicho and had him murdered. Immediately the army of the West dissolved, the Visigoths entered Italy and in 410 took Rome by storm. Tribes of Germans were now loose all over the West. In theory an emperor still ruled and by encouraging Germans to fight one another he could sometimes impose some order on the situation. But the real power lay with the German tribes.

Through all this the Huns had been remarkably quiet. Then in 433 they acquired a new king who reckoned that what the Germans could do he could do better. This was Attila, 'the scourge of God'. He struck the East first and only withdrew when the court of Constantinople had paid over all its gold and promised to dismantle its fortifications on the Danube. Then he moved west, frightening even more Germans into the empire. For ten years he terrorized the whole area between the Rhine, the Balkans and the Caucasus.

In 451 he advanced into France. Though the Visigoths claimed to have defeated him near Troyes it was the Visigothic king that was killed in the battle. In 452 he invaded northern Italy and devastated the Po valley. Then Attila died. His empire disintegrated immediately. Quarrelling among themselves the various Hun tribes withdrew to the Russian steppe.

So the Huns never created more than a temporary tribute-levying empire in Europe – nothing to match the long-lived empire of the Turks in north China. But they did push the Germans into destroying the western half of the Roman Empire. This event may have been inevitable and overdue but it was none the less a turning point. The sack of Rome by Alaric, king of the Visigoths, marks the end of the classical world and the beginning of Europe's Dark Ages.

---

[1] Stilicho was by birth a Vandal. During the 4th century the Romans had come to rely more and more on German mercenaries, and by its end Germans had risen to the highest commands.

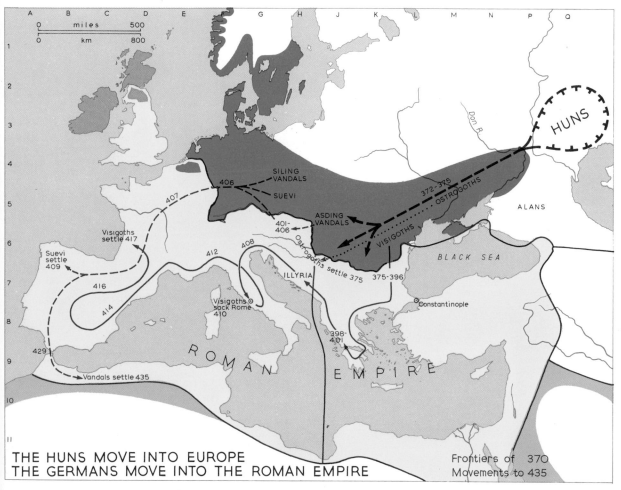

THE HUNS MOVE INTO EUROPE
THE GERMANS MOVE INTO THE ROMAN EMPIRE

Frontiers of 370
Movements to 435

Map 1 labels:

HUNS

SILING VANDALS
SUEVI
ASDING VANDALS
401-406
406
372-375 OSTROGOTHS
VISIGOTHS
ALANS

407
Visigoths settle 417
Suevi settle 409
416
414
412
408
Ostrogoths settle 375
375-396
ILLYRIA
BLACK SEA

Visigoths sack Rome 410
Constantinople

429
398-401
Vandals settle 435

R O M A N   E M P I R E

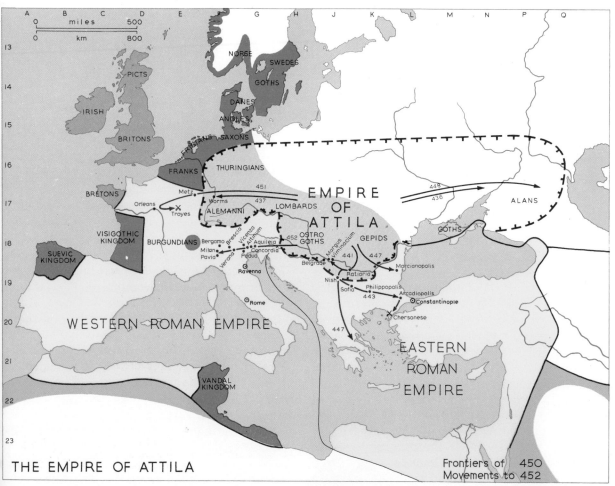

THE EMPIRE OF ATTILA

Frontiers of 450
Movements to 452

Map 2 labels:

NORSE
SWEDES
GOTHS
DANES
PICTS
IRISH
BRITONS
ANGLES
SAXONS
FRISIANS
THURINGIANS
FRANKS
BRETONS
Metz
Orleans
Worms
Troyes
ALEMANNI
451
437
LOMBARDS
EMPIRE OF ATTILA
448
436
ALANS
GOTHS

VISIGOTHIC KINGDOM
SUEVIC KINGDOM
BURGUNDIANS
Bergamo Brescia Vicenza Altinum
Milan Pavia Verona Padua Concordia Aquileia
452 OSTRO GOTHS
Marcus Viminacium
441 GEPIDS 447
Ravenna
Belgrade
Ratiaria Marcianopolis
Rome
Nish
Sofia Philippopolis Arcadiopolis
443 Constantinople
447 Chersonese

WESTERN ROMAN EMPIRE

EASTERN ROMAN EMPIRE

VANDAL KINGDOM

9

The German Kingdoms 450-510

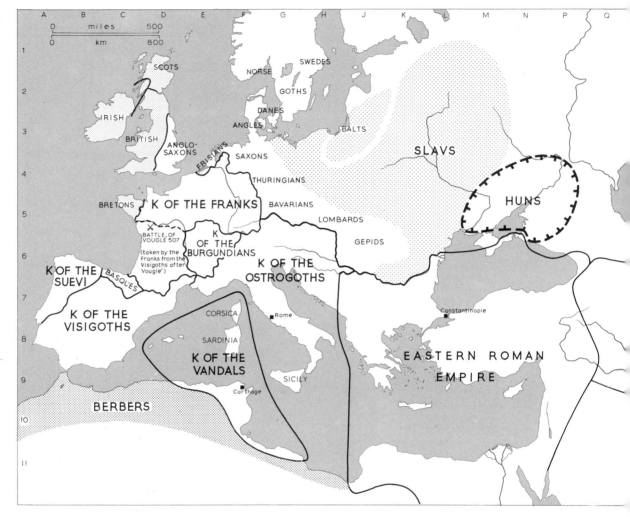

Of the German tribes loose inside the Roman Empire it was the Vandals who caused the most spectacular trouble.

From Spain they crossed to Africa where they moved along the coast to Carthage. Once they were masters of this famous port, the Vandals built up a formidable fleet and raided round the shores of the Mediterranean. They plundered many important towns, including Rome (455). They conquered Corsica, Sardinia and the western end of Sicily. The Vandal kingdom now looked very like the Carthaginian empire of a thousand years earlier. But the ancient Carthaginians had been traders; the Vandals were simply pirates.

The rest of the Western Empire mostly fell into the hands of the Goths. In the 470s the Visigoths expanded their kingdom in France and conquered three quarters of Spain. At this time the Ostrogoths were still in the Eastern Empire. To get rid of them the Eastern emperor suggested that they march against the West (the proposal that had got rid of the Visigoths). The Ostrogothic king Theodoric liked the idea and managed to conquer Italy from the miscellaneous Germans who were occupying it.[1]

Besides the Goths and Vandals there were the Franks. Clovis, king of the Franks, took all of France that the Visigoths hadn't. In 505 he conquered the Alemanni. And in 507 he defeated the Visigoths themselves and ran them almost out of France. Theodoric intervened and the balance between the three main German kingdoms seemed restored. But the real balance was between Frank and Ostrogoth, between Clovis and Theodoric.

[1] They had deposed the last emperor of the West in 476.

Ravenna 404-752

When bad times started for the Western Empire the emperor Honorius moved to Ravenna, a little town at the southern point of the Po delta. The marshes that surrounded Ravenna made it easy to defend.

Ravenna remained the capital of Italy under the Gothic kings and, after Justinian's reconquest, under the Byzantine governors. It never grew very big – about as big as Byzantium before Septimius Severus enlarged it – and became a backwater when Byzantine rule in Italy collapsed. So it has preserved many of its 5th- and 6th-century churches intact.

During the Dark Ages Ravenna and Rome were almost the only places in western Europe where there was any building in permanent materials – brick or stone. So the churches of Ravenna are remarkable in that they exist at all. They are even more remarkable for their superb mosaics. The Romans had developed the art of mosaic work over many centuries. It reached its peak in Ravenna during the period of the Goths and the first Byzantine governors.

Honorius built his palace to the north of Roman Ravenna, Theodoric built his on the far side of the Via Popilia, the coast road that ran to the east of the town. Soon a score of little bridges spanned the canal that divided the palaces from the town and new buildings filled the open spaces between. A new wall was built around the whole complex. Its peculiar outline reflects the haphazard relationship between the original Roman grid, the area of Honorius' palace and the ribbon development along the Via Popilia.

7 Maximian, Archbishop of Ravenna 546–52

10 *far right* The tomb of Theodoric. Its vault is a single stone weighing 300 tons

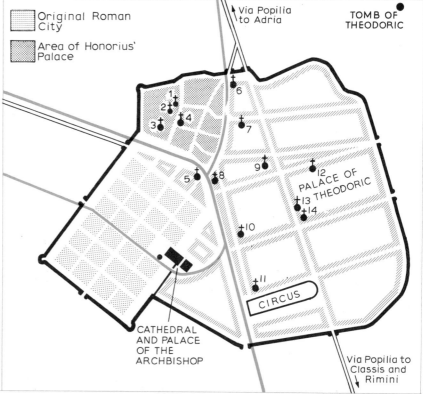

Original Roman City

Area of Honorius' Palace

Via Popilia to Adria

TOMB OF THEODORIC

PALACE OF THEODORIC

CIRCUS

CATHEDRAL AND PALACE OF THE ARCHBISHOP

Via Popilia to Classis and Rimini

8 and 9 Contrasting styles of church architecture: the octagonal S. Vitale in Ravenna (3 on the map) and the basilica of S. Apollinare in Classis (4 km south of Ravenna). The difference between these types of church is explained on p. 27

1 S. Croce
2 Mausoleum of Galla Placidia
3 S. Vitale
4 S. Maria Maggiore
5 S. Domenico
6 S. Vittore
7 S. Giovanni Battista
8 S. Michele in Afficisio
9 Spirito Santo
10 S. Francesco
11 S. Eufemia
12 S. Giovanni Evangelista
13 S. Apollinare Nuovo
14 S. Salvatore

Justinian 527-565

11 Justinian

In 527 Justinian became emperor of the Eastern Roman Empire. His ambition was to reconquer the lost western provinces.

His cabinet thought the task was hopeless and voted unanimously against his plans. Justinian went ahead anyway. He put his trust in a young general named Belisarius, who had distinguished himself in a recent war with Persia. Belisarius had fought off a superior Persian army by entrenching his infantry (mostly local militia) and using his cavalry to worry the flanks of the enemy attack. The battle of Daras had not been a crushing victory but it had shown that Belisarius could do a great deal with a very few good troops.

Justinian first sent Belisarius against the Vandals. He gave him 16,000 men, which was about as big as armies came in those days. Sailing via Sicily by courtesy of the Ostrogoths, his expedition completely surprised the enemy. Half the Vandal army was putting down a revolt in Sardinia: the half still at home was defeated and dispersed by Belisarius outside Carthage. When the other half came back from Sardinia he annihilated this, too. The Vandal king surrendered and, after taking possession of various Vandal outposts, Belisarius returned to Constantinople in triumph.

In 535 Justinian sent Belisarius west again, this time to fight the Ostrogoths. King Theodoric was dead and the Gothic power was weakening fast but even so Justinian was remarkably confident. He gave Belisarius only half the number of soldiers he had had for his African expedition. Belisarius certainly got off to a flying start. Sicily submitted on his arrival – the only fighting was at Palermo – and even when he moved to the mainland (536) he met no effective opposition until Naples. The siege of Naples took only three weeks: by the end of the year Belisarius had been welcomed into Rome by cheering crowds.

The citizens would have cheered less loudly if they had known what was in Belisarius' mind. He had decided to sit tight in Rome and leave the next move to the Goths. He put his men to work repairing the city wall. When the main Gothic army arrived the city was too strong to be taken by assault. The Goths had to try a siege – and Rome was too big to encircle.[1]

The siege lasted a year. Belisarius used the northern semicircle of the city wall rather as he had the entrenchments at Daras -- as protection for his infantry. Whenever there was an opportunity he sent his cavalry out to cut up isolated Gothic units. Gradually he wore down the superior numbers and the morale of his opponents.

When the Goths withdrew Belisarius took the offensive again. Justinian sent out reinforcements and, in 539, a second small army which landed at Ancona on the Adriatic coast. Belisarius began to close in on Ravenna. The approach required slow siege work, but when a third imperial army marched round the head of the Adriatic the military and diplomatic pressure grew too much for the dispirited Goths. In 540 the Ostrogothic king surrendered himself and his capital. Belisarius was able to return to the East with another captive monarch in his train. Small Ostrogothic forces remained at large in the Po valley but it looked as though a last push would complete the job.

Unfortunately the Ostrogoths failed to collapse as expected. They elected a new king named Totila who restored their morale by a series of successful offensives. In 544 Belisarius returned to Italy to find Roman rule disintegrating everywhere. This time he had with him a mere 4000 men and there was little he could do but fight a losing version of his old chess-board tactics. By 551 he had nothing left but Ravenna and Ancona – the Goths were raiding Sicily, Sardinia and the Balkan coast.

In 552 Justinian managed to scrape up a new army large enough to face the Goths in the field. He entrusted it not to Belisarius whose reputation was now tarnished but to Narses, the Court Chamberlain. It was a surprisingly good choice. Narses collected a strong contingent of Lombards as he marched round the head of the Adriatic to Ravenna.[2] From there he advanced on Rome. At Busta Gallorum on the Via Flaminia (the

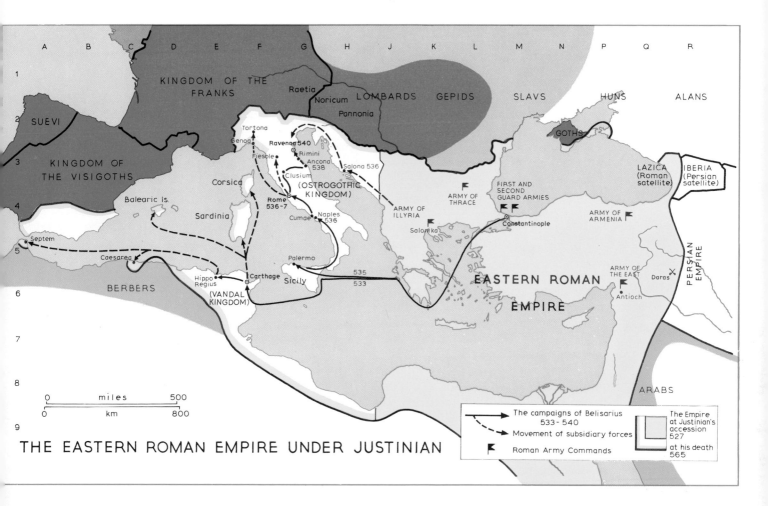

THE EASTERN ROMAN EMPIRE UNDER JUSTINIAN

Map labels:
KINGDOM OF THE FRANKS
Raetia
Noricum
LOMBARDS
GEPIDS
SLAVS
HUNS
ALANS
SUEVI
Pannonia
GOTHS
KINGDOM OF THE VISIGOTHS
LAZICA (Roman satellite)
IBERIA (Persian satellite)
Tortona
Genoa
Ravenna 540
Fiesole
Rimini
Ancona 538
Corsica
Clusium
Salona 536
Balearic Is.
Rome 536-7
(OSTROGOTHIC KINGDOM)
ARMY OF THRACE
FIRST AND SECOND GUARD ARMIES
ARMY OF ARMENIA
Sardinia
Naples 536
Cumae
ARMY OF ILLYRIA
Septem
Salonika
Constantinople
PERSIAN EMPIRE
Caesarea
Palermo
EASTERN ROMAN EMPIRE
ARMY OF THE EAST
Daras
Hippo Regius
Carthage
Sicily
535
533
Antioch
BERBERS
(VANDAL KINGDOM)
ARABS

miles 0 500
km 0 800

Legend:
→ The campaigns of Belisarius 533-540
--→ Movement of subsidiary forces
⚐ Roman Army Commands
☐ The Empire at Justinian's accession 527
☐ at his death 565

highway across the Apennines) Goth and Roman met for what both sides recognized to be the decisive battle of the long war.

The result was a complete victory for the Romans. The attacking Goths were trapped by the Roman centre and destroyed by the fire of the bowmen Narses had massed on the flanks. Totila was among the Gothic dead. Next year Narses killed Totila's successor as he was vainly trying to break through to Cumae and the Gothic treasure. We know of no more kings of the Ostrogoths and, though some Goths held out for a while in the north, the restoration of Roman power now proceeded steadily. Within a decade all Italy was once more within the empire.[3]

The African and Italian campaigns were not the only wars Justinian waged. He had to hold off the Persians, to defend the Balkans against German and Slav raids and turn the Berbers out of the parts of Roman Africa they had occupied during the Vandal decline. All of these he did more or less successfully. He also sent a small expedition against the Visigoths of Spain which won him the southeast of the country. In sum, he held

the East and reconquered about a third of the West.

Whether it was all worth while has always been argued. Procopius, Justinian's official historian, thought not. He closes his account of the African wars with the sentence: 'So it came about that those of the Africans who survived, few as they were in number and exceedingly poor, at last and after great trial, found some peace.' The implication is that the reconquered provinces were too devastated to be worth anything to the empire. But the truth is probably that the western provinces had long since disintegrated socially (which is why the Western Empire had collapsed in the first place) and that in this state they had nothing to contribute to the upkeep of the empire anyway.

[1] The total circuit is 18 km.
[2] Narses' march is not shown on the map.
[3] Justinian did not attempt to occupy the old Roman provinces of the middle Danube which had been part of Theodoric's kingdom. The Bavarians in Raetia became independent; Noricum and Pannonia were left for the Lombards who moved in with Justinian's blessing (545).

Constantinople
324-600

Constantinople was not the first city to stand beside the Golden Horn. On its site an earlier city, Byzantium, had been founded by Greeks from Megara in 660 BC.

Over the centuries Byzantium prospered, never quite making the first rank but always comfortably in the second. In AD 193–6 it chose the wrong side in one of the Roman Empire's civil wars and was sacked by the victor, Septimius Severus. However, Severus soon relented and rebuilt the city bigger than it had been before. In 323–4 the Byzantines made the same lucky mistake. This time the victor was the emperor Constantine the Great, protector of the persecuted Christians. He decided to make Byzantium his capital and a city to rival Rome itself. Byzantium was transformed into Constantinople, the city of Constantine.[1]

Rome was built on seven hills and divided into fourteen districts. With a little imagination it was possible to see seven hills in and around Byzantium and it was a simple administrative act to divide the new Rome into fourteen districts. Actually the 13th and 14th districts were not really part of Constantine's city. The 13th was the village of Sykae (later known as Galata) on the opposite side of the Golden Horn, and the 14th the settlement of Blachernae at the south end of the wooden bridge over the Horn.[2]

Constantine reserved the whole first district for the imperial palace. This was not a palace in our sense but a sort of sprawling luxury village. Reception rooms and private apartments were built as one-storey pavilions. In between were courts and gardens, offices and guard rooms, a number of court churches (eventually half a dozen) and a polo ground. Nothing of this survives, but the Seraglio – the palace which the Turkish sultans later built in the 2nd district (the site of old Byzantium) – gives some idea of how the imperial palace must have looked in its heyday.

Within a century the city outgrew Constantine's walls and a new wall was built to defend the suburbs. The north end of the wall incorporated the fortifications of Blachernae which now became a proper part of the city. This was Constantinople's final wall and is the one illustrated on the title-page. The defences were completed by sea walls which ran all round the rest of the city.

With the decline of Rome in the 5th century Constantinople became the biggest city in the world. At its peak it held anything between 100,000 and 250,000 people – more than twice as many as Alexandria and three times as many as Antioch. The only cities to rival it were the capital cities of China.

[1] Since the Turkish conquest in 1453 it has been known as Istanbul.
[2] This bridge disappears early on in the capital's history, presumably destroyed by attackers or defenders in one of the assaults on the city

The main forum (public square) of Constantinople was the Augusteum. On three of its sides this had the cathedral of S. Sophia, the Senate and the entrance to the Hippodrome (the stadium for the chariot racing which was the citizens' passion). The entrance to the imperial palace area lay between the last two. From the fourth side ran the city's main street, the Mese or 'middle way'.

In the centre of the Augusteum (named for Constantine's mother, Augusta Helena) was the milion, the milestone from which all distances within the Eastern Empire were measured.

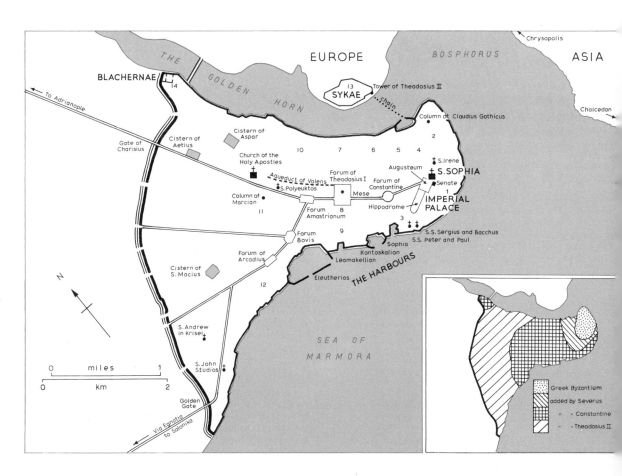

Constantinople's most famous building has always been its cathedral, S. Sophia. The first church of this name was built by Constantine and his son Constantius. It burnt down in the reign of Justinian who is responsible for the present building.

S. Sophia is a complicated building as well as a big one but its basic plan is simple – one square inside another. The central square is roofed with a high dome: the outer square is formed by the addition of a two-storey walk-round.

S. Sophia's dome is carried by four big arches which transmit its weight to the massive brick piers at the corners of the inner square. The architects expected this inner unit (12A) to be stable on its own.

To get to 12B means adding the walk-round on two sides and filling in the big arches on these sides with rows of columns (at ground and gallery levels) and windows (on the two levels above the gallery). The front and back are now finished in a more complicated way. A half-dome turns the central space into an oblong. The inner dotted line on the floor of 12B shows the effect of this on the plan. Then three little half-domes are let into each big one. The outer dotted line gives the final shape.

Justinian was very pleased with his new cathedral. 'Solomon, I have surpassed you' he said when he first entered it.

What the architects had not allowed for was that a dome exerts sideways as well as downwards pressure. The sideways pressure slowly pushed the tops of the piers apart. Twenty years after the church was completed they were so far apart that the dome fell in (558). Justinian had a new dome built and this time the piers were buttressed. More buttresses have had to be added every few hundred years since then and even so the dome has partly collapsed twice more (in 989 and 1346).

This is a poor record compared to the dome of the Pantheon.[1] It has to be admitted that the East Romans did not have the old Romans' touch for engineering. But whereas in the Pantheon there is really nothing to look at except a dome of staggering size, the half-domes and galleries of S. Sophia change its shape for you with every step you take. The Pantheon is a perfect design: S. Sophia is a perfect composition.

13 *Above* S. Sophia seen across the piazza which occupies the site of the old hippodrome. One of the huge arches that support the dome is clearly visible between the projecting buttresses. The minarets were, of course, added by the Turks.

The obelisk in the foreground originally stood in Heliopolis in Egypt where it had been put up by Tutmosis III in 1450 BC. It was brought to Constantinople by Theodosius I in 390. The stick of barley-sugar inside the circular railing is the stump of the Serpent Column, a victory trophy put up by the Greeks at Delphi in 480 BC. Constantine the Great brought it to Constantinople.

Though the level of the ground is now about 4.5 m higher than it was in Justinian's day the piazza still keeps the outline of the hippodrome, while the obelisk and the Serpent Column give the position of its *spina* – the wall down the middle round which the chariots raced.

14 The only part of the Imperial palace to survive, the underground reservoir built by Justinian. Its brick vaults are carried by 336 columns

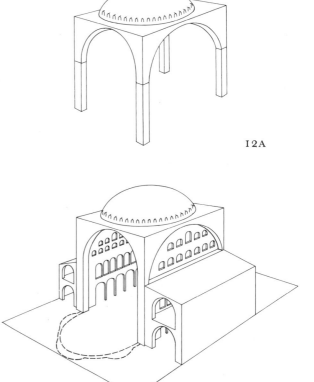

12A

12B

[1] The dome of the Pantheon despite its much larger diameter (43.2 m against 32 m) has stayed up since it was built in 118–28. In fairness it should be said that the dome of S. Sophia gets into trouble because the piers that carry it are so high: the dome rises to 56 m above floor level while the Pantheon has a height merely equal to its diameter

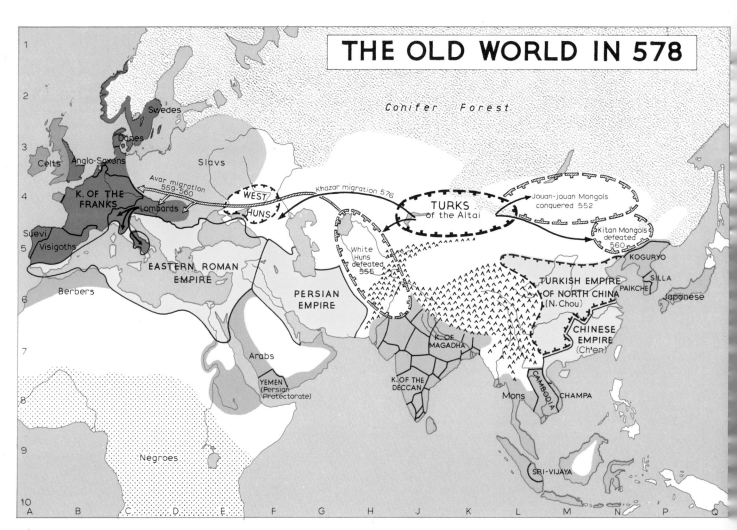

The Turks of the Altai 550-580

While the Turks of the Inner Mongolian steppe were conquering the north half of China, the Turks of Outer Mongolia lived a quiet life herding their flocks on the slopes of the Altai mountains.

Like the White Huns to their west they paid tribute to the lords of the outer steppe, the Jouan-jouan Mongols. That is, they did until 552 when they turned on their masters, totally defeated them and became lords of the steppe themselves. To the east they swept on as far as the borders of Manchuria where they defeated the Kitan Mongols. To the west they overthrew the White Huns and sent them flying off into Europe.[1]

By the time these fugitive White Huns arrived in Europe they had been joined by other defeated groups of nomads and acquired the new name of Avars (nobody knows why). The Avars conquered the Huns and Slavs of the Russian steppe, defeated the Franks in central Germany and pushed the Lombards out of Pannonia into Italy. The Lombards quickly overran most of the Italian province that Justinian had gone to such pains to recover.

The victories won by the Turks of the Altai had no effect on their way of life: they remained herdsmen and warriors. You could not say the same about the Turks who ruled north China. They had conquered not empty plains but a land teeming with people. They had become aristocrats ruling over China's peasants. Gradually they dropped Turkish habits in favour of Chinese; in the end they became completely Chinese in manners and outlook. The start of a new dynasty, the Sui, in 580 marks the point where the empire of north China must be called Chinese, not Turkish. In fact it soon became the only Chinese empire, for in 589 the Sui completed the conquest of the south and brought the whole country under one rule again.

[1] In the 5th century the White Huns had destroyed the Kushan kingdom and then become the terror of north India just as the western Huns had destroyed the Ostrogothic kingdom of south Russia and then become the terror of Europe. The White Hun equivalent of Attila was Miharagula. The Gupta Empire completely disintegrated under his attacks and even after the White Hun Empire had been destroyed by the Turks, the Ganges valley remained broken up into a dozen or more quarrelling states.

15 Turkish lancer

THE OLD WORLD IN 578

The Lombards in Italy 568-700

16 Lombard cavalryman

The Lombards moved into Italy in 568. They had learned the way when they marched with Narses' army fifteen years before. Now, with the Avars breathing down their necks, an invasion of Italy seemed a better idea than staying where they were.

It was. Without a battle the Lombards made themselves masters of the Po valley. This became the heart of their kingdom and has ever since been known as Lombardy. Then they moved south, conquering most of the interior of the peninsula. But if the east Romans in Italy were too weak to face the Lombards in the field they still had command of the sea. Their garrisons hung on in the walled towns on or near the coast. The result was the peculiar division shown on the map.[1]

This division lasted a surprisingly long time. The only changes in the 7th century were the Lombard conquests of Genoa and most of the heel of the peninsula. The Lombards failed to complete the conquest of Italy because the Lombard king had to spend most of his time trying to keep order among his dukes.

There were about thirty dukes. The two in the south – the dukes of Spoleto and Benevento – had deliberately left the corridor between Rome and Ravenna unconquered so that the Lombard king could not get at them at all. In the north there were another five – the ones marked on the map – who were able to do pretty much as they liked, whatever the king said.

The Lombards were not the only people to move as a result of Avar pressure. Shortly after the Avars arrived in Europe the Slavs of the Upper Danube region began to press into the northern Balkans. While the east Romans held the Lower Danube, which they did throughout the 6th century, the Slav movement was limited. But Slav tribes (probably under Avar suzerainty) gradually occupied the northern half of what is now Yugoslavia. By the opening years of the 7th century the Romans controlled only the coastal province of Dalmatia. Even this was shrinking fast: soon 'Dalmatia' was down to three or four towns on the Adriatic coast.

The Romans called the heel of Italy Calabria and the toe Bruttii. When the Lombards conquered the heel the Romans transferred the name Calabria to the toe: it has meant the toe ever since.

Transferring the name of a lost province to the nearest area still within the Empire was something the Romans had done before and would do again. It makes the geography of the Empire confusing but presumably enabled the Romans to pretend that the Empire was as big as ever, as well as providing readymade jobs for the displaced administrators.

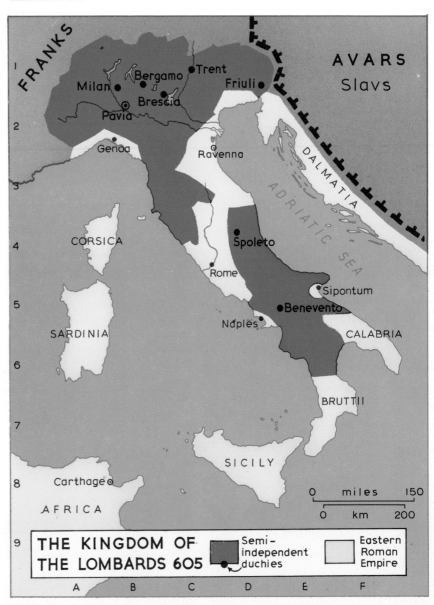

THE KINGDOM OF THE LOMBARDS 605

Semi-independent duchies

Eastern Roman Empire

FRANKS

Milan · Bergamo · Trent
Brescia
Pavia
Genoa
Ravenna

AVARS
Slavs
Friuli
DALMATIA
ADRIATIC SEA

CORSICA

Spoleto
Rome
Sipontum
Benevento
Naples
CALABRIA

SARDINIA

BRUTTII

SICILY

Carthage
AFRICA

0 miles 150
0 km 200

---

[1] Constantinople appointed a viceroy – the exarch of Ravenna – to run the Italian provinces (except Sicily). He had authority over both civil and military personnel, which was unheard of in the normal Roman administrative system. A second exarch was appointed for the African provinces (plus Corsica and Sardinia). The creation of these special exarchates suggests that Constantinople had decided not to use eastern armies again in the West: the reconquered provinces would have to fend for themselves.

Rome: the Pope takes over 400-600

Rome remained a great city for a century after its sack by the Visigoths. Though not as big as it had been it was still bigger than any other city in the west. The collapse came during Justinian's war of reconquest. In that twenty-year struggle the city changed hands five times. The population sank to a few thousand.

The Pope kept Rome going – he had no alternative if the Papacy was to survive. He brought food in from the Church's estates in Italy and Sicily and slowly the population built up again to 10,000–15,000 (at which it remained for the rest of the Dark Ages). This was less than a tenth of what it had been, so most of the city decayed into rubble.

The map shows Rome as it was in the days of Pope Gregory the Great (590–604). He was really civil governor of the city as well as Pope: the Byzantines withdrew their garrison soon after the Lombards invaded Italy. The Pope lived in the Lateran Palace (originally a gift of the emperor Constantine); the Lateran basilica of St John was the city's cathedral.

There were twenty-five parish churches, most of them built in the last century of the empire, plus a dozen other churches founded for special reasons. For example, S. Maria Maggiore had been built by Sixtus III in 432–40 after the decision of the Council of Ephesus that Mary was the Mother of God and not just the mother of Christ's human body. S. Agata had been built by the Goths (who held the opposite view of Mary, a heresy known as Arianism). S. Croce in the Sessorian Palace was originally the private chapel of the emperors. S. Maria in Cosmedin was the church of the Greek colony.

Outside the walls were more churches, many of them bigger than those inside. These were built over the places where the early martyrs had been buried (Roman law forbade burial within the walls). Naturally, the biggest were those over the graves of the apostles Peter and Paul. Eventually St Peter's was to replace St John-in-Lateran as the main church of Rome.

THE PARISH CHURCHES

1	S. Anastasia	B2
2	S. Balbina	B3
3	S. Cecilia	A2
4	S. Clemente	C2
5	S. Crisogono	A2
6	S. Cyriaci	C1
7	S. Eusebio	C1
8	SS. Giovanni e Paolo	B2
9	S. Lorenzo in Damaso	A1
10	S. Lorenzo in Lucina	B1
11	S. Marcello	B1
12	S. Marco	B2
13	S. Maria in Trastevere	A2
14	S. Martino ai Monti	C2
15	SS. Nereo ed Achilleo	C3
16	SS. Pietro e Marcellino	C2
17	S. Pietro in Vincoli	B2
18	S. Prassede	C2
19	S. Prisca	B3
20	S. Pudenziana	C1
21	Quattro Coronati	C2
22	S. Sabina	B3
23	S. Sisto Vecchio	C3
24	S. Susannae	B1
25	S. Vitale	B1

Since Gregory the Great's time most of these have been rebuilt several times over and some have been resited but only 6 and 24 have vanished completely. The best preserved is S. Sabina (22) which still looks much as it did in late Roman times. S. Balbina (2) and S. Pudenziana (20) are also substantially intact and you can visit the original S. Clemente (4) underneath the present-day (12th century) basilica.

Crisis in the East 600-628

17 Heraclius, East Roman emperor
610–41, with his sons
Constantine III and Heraclonas

18 Chosroes II, king
of Persia 590–628

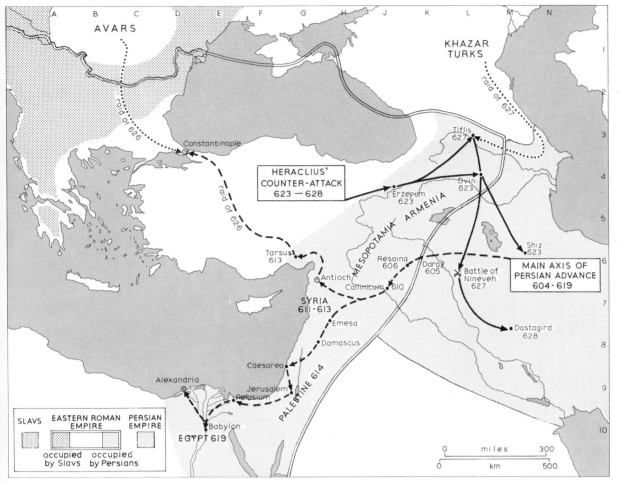

Though the year 600 saw the Eastern Roman Empire in trouble in Italy, it looked as strong as ever in the east.

The Persians had agreed to frontier changes that were all in Constantinople's favour. In the Balkans the Roman army was harrying the Avars and Slavs. But in 602 this army rebelled, marched on Constantinople and put its general, Phocas, on the imperial throne. Phocas' reign was a disaster. First, the Slavs rolled over the Balkans in what was more a migration than an invasion. The European quarter of the empire shrank to the coastline.

Then the Persians broke down the defences of Mesopotamia and burst through to Antioch. They went on to conquer all the provinces cut off by this attack – Syria, Palestine and Egypt. The empire was now reduced to Anatolia, Constantinople, a few towns in the Balkans and some scattered provinces (North Africa, bits of Italy, the Mediter-ranean islands and a slice of Spain) too far away to be much help.

The exarch of Africa did send one important aid, his son, who took over as the emperor Heraclius (610). He reorganized what was left of the Empire, licked what was left of the army into shape and then marched into Armenia.[1]

He had been campaigning there for four years without much success when the Persians and Avars decided to make a joint attack on Constantinople. The Roman fleet kept the Persians and Avars apart and the attack was a failure (626). The next year Heraclius' strategy paid off: with a bit of help from the Khazar Turks he broke out of Armenia, moved across the Persians' supply line and brought them to battle near Nineveh. He won the battle and the war. The Persians sued for peace (628): the lost eastern provinces were returned. Heraclius had saved the empire.

[1] Heraclius' administrative reorganization is dealt with on p. 48. It was so far-reaching that historians call the post-Heraclian empire by a new name – the Byzantine Empire.

The name was chosen because one of Heraclius' changes was to stop the official use of Latin (which few of his subjects spoke) in favour of Greek (which nearly all of them did) and Byzantium was what the Greeks had called the forerunner of Constantinople. Byzantine is a useful word but it is worth remembering that the 'Byzantines' never used it: right to the end they called their city Constantinople and themselves and their empire Roman.

Arabia and Mohammed
500-632

19 'In the name of God the merciful, the compassionate' – the beginning of the oldest Islamic inscription known, a tombstone dated AH 31 (AD 652)

For most people the word Arabia conjures up a picture of camels, Bedouin and desert. Certainly much of Arabia is desert, some of it as lifeless as the Sahara, but by no means all of it is like that.

The mountainous rim of the peninsula catches enough rainfall to allow regular agriculture at the corners – in Oman and, more important, the Yemen. And along the western side oases have formed where dips in the hills collect enough rain. The caravans that carried incense from the Yemen to the temples of the Mediterranean world were able to thread their way from one oasis-village to another as they passed through this area. So it is called the Hejaz, 'the Corridor'.

Probably half the one or two million inhabitants of 6th-century Arabia lived in Oman, the Yemen or the Hejaz. The rest were Bedouin herdsmen who bred camels, sheep and goats in the areas round the oases, on the central plateau (Najd) or on the fringes of Palestine and Iraq. The Bedouin were few and scattered but Arabia is a big place and they occupied all of it except the absolute deserts – the Nefud and the Rub al Khali ('the Empty Quarter'). They were used to moving in search of their pasture: if someone could get them all to move together he would have a formidable force at his disposal.

In the oasis-villages of Arabia were the temples of the local gods. The Bedouin would worship at these shrines when they came to market. The general Arab view was that people should be loyal to their local gods, but that other people's gods deserved respect too. In the 6th century less tolerant faiths such as Judaism and Christianity filtered along the caravan routes and some of the townspeople became Jews or Christians. But most of the Bedouin remained faithful to the old gods.

A major success for Christianity at this time was the conversion of Abyssinia. Originally a Yemenite colony, Abyssinia had grown over the centuries until it was stronger than the disunited Yemen. The Abyssinian king now declared himself the protector of Christians in Arabia and when the Bedouin massacred a number of them he sent an expedition to extract vengeance. This destroyed the Kaaba (temple) of Nejra, the most famous pagan shrine in all Arabia. It also established an Abyssinian as governor of the southwest.

After Nejra the most important temple was at Mecca, in the Hejaz. The guardians of this temple were an Arab clan called the Quraish. In 570 the Abyssinian governor of the Yemen decided to attack the Meccan Kaaba. An elephant, guaranteed to strike terror into all who saw it, was sent over from Abyssinia for the expedition. The Quraish abandoned Mecca and took to the hills but the blow never fell. Decimated by an attack of the plague, the Abyssinians turned back. The Quraish jubilantly claimed a miracle.

It was in Mecca in 'The Year of the Elephant' that the Prophet Mohammed was born. A member of the Quraish, though not an important one, he lived quite obscurely until, at the age of forty, he started to have visions of God. As a result he began to preach a new religion: Islam.

From the Jews he took the doctrine of one God only, the Jewish series of prophets and a hatred of idols. From the Christians he borrowed Christ, but as a prophet not a God. From the superstitions of the Bedouin he accepted little more than the special holiness of the Meccan Kaaba – and at first he was dubious about that. He demanded obedience from his followers in everything but never claimed that he himself was more than a man, though a divinely inspired one. The heart of his message was simple: 'There is no God but God and Mohammed is His Prophet.' Anyone who repeated this formula was a Moslem – Islam itself simply means 'submission'.

Mohammed's preaching had little success in Mecca and aroused great antagonism among his fellow Quraish. But he did make converts among the pilgrims visiting the Kaaba and when, twelve years after his first vision, he had to flee for safety he chose Yathrib, a city 350 km to the north where he had built up a following.[1]

The addition of his few Meccan supporters gave Mohammed control of Yathrib and his teaching now took on an aggressive note. He broke with the local Jews and expelled them. He raided the caravans of the Meccans. He promised eternal paradise to any believer who fell in battle against the infidel. But the Meccans were not intimidated. Led by the Umayyad branch of the Quraish, they defeated the Mohammedans and nearly managed to take Yathrib. It was Mohammed's success in winning over the Bedouin that finally tipped the scales. What use was possession of the Kaaba if the

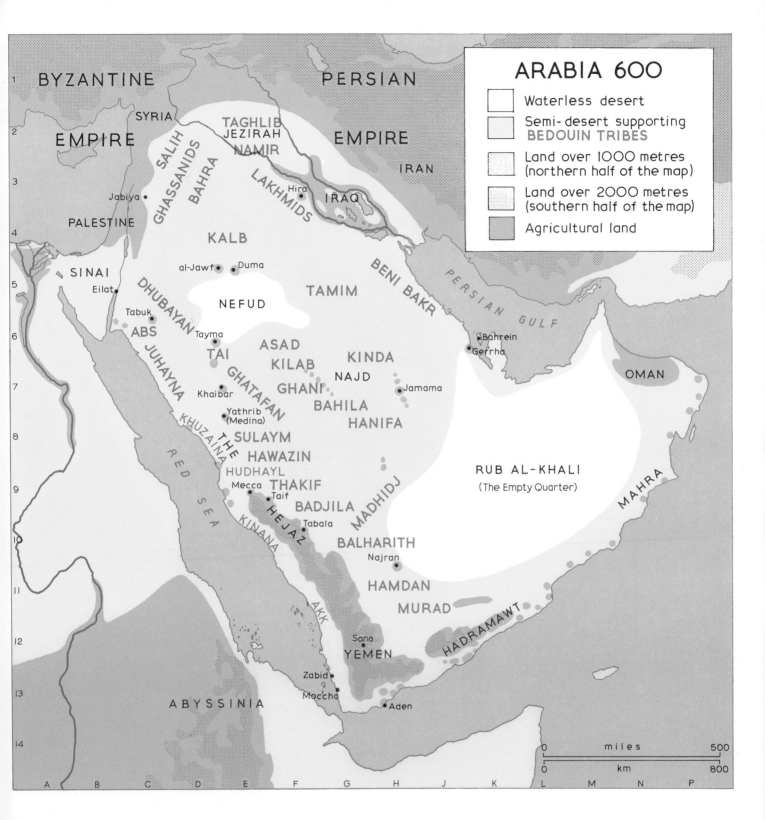

ARABIA 600

Waterless desert

Semi-desert supporting
BEDOUIN TRIBES

Land over 1000 metres
(northern half of the map)

Land over 2000 metres
(southern half of the map)

Agricultural land

BYZANTINE

EMPIRE

SYRIA

PALESTINE

SINAI

Jabiya

Eilat

Tabuk

PERSIAN

EMPIRE

IRAN

IRAQ

Hira

TAGHLIB
JEZIRAH
NAMIR

SALIH
GHASSANIDS
BAHRA

LAKHMIDS

KALB

al-Jawf   Duma

NEFUD

TAMIM

BENI BAKR

DHUBAYAN

ABS

Tayma

TAI

JUHAYNA

KHUZAINA

THE

SULAYM

HAWAZIN

HUDHAYL

Mecca

THAKIF

Taif

HEJAZ

BADJILA

Tabala

KINANA

AKK

ASAD

KILAB

GHATAFAN

GHANI

Khaibar

Yathrib
(Medina)

NAJD

KINDA

BAHILA

HANIFA

Jamama

MADHIDJ

BALHARITH

Najran

HAMDAN

MURAD

Sana

YEMEN

Zabid

Moccha

ABYSSINIA

Aden

PERSIAN GULF

Bahrein

Gerrha

OMAN

RUB AL-KHALI
(The Empty Quarter)

MAHRA

HADRAMAWT

RED SEA

miles   500

km   800

pilgrims no longer came? After eight years, the Meccans capitulated. In 630 Mohammed entered the Kaaba and destroyed the idols it contained. Even the Umayyads embraced Islam.

The Prophet lived for two more years. He returned to Yathrib (henceforth known as Medina – which simply means 'the city') and there received and accepted into Islam delegates from all parts of the Arabian peninsula.[2]

[1] From this flight (Hegira) dates the Moslem era: Year 1 runs from summer AD 622 to summer AD 623. But the year is not a true

year, because like many other primitive peoples the Arabs had constructed their calendar by observing the moon instead of the sun.

The moon goes round the earth a bit less than 12½ times a year. Consequently a calendar based on 12 lunar months is 11 days short. You can get a fairly accurate calendar by adding a day to each month. Alternatively you can add an extra month every third year. Qusai, the Quraish leader who seized the Meccan Kaaba in 440, put the Meccans on the extra-month system. But Mohammed, for reasons unknown, went back to the simple lunar calendar. So every Moslem year the seasons arrive 11 days earlier and a Moslem century is completed after only 97 real years.

[2] The Yemenites had expelled the Abyssinians with the help of the Persians in 574. The Persians established a sort of control there till 605.

The Arab Conquests
633-653

20 Arab horse-archer

After Mohammed's death his father-in-law Abu Bekr was recognized by the elders of Medina as caliph ('successor'). Abu Bekr's first action was to mount a series of quick campaigns to enforce Islam throughout Arabia. A year saw this done. Then, as the Prophet had intended, the Bedouin armies were sent north against Byzantium and Persia.

The two main armies made for the grazing country on the borders of Syria and Iraq. These pastoral areas were normally held by Arab tribes – the beni Ghassan and Lakhmids who were vassals of Byzantium and Persia respectively. Now they were occupied by the armies of Islam as they tested the defences of the agricultural zone.

On the Syrian front the Arabs broke through to Damascus in 635. The next year, when the main Byzantine army arrived, they retreated and it was at the River Yarmuk that the decisive battle was fought. The result was an Arab victory so overwhelming that the Byzantines abandoned Syria to them. Palestine was now cut off – the small Arab force that was operating there was able to take Jerusalem in 637. By then the main army was moving north against the chain of Byzantine fortresses in north Mesopotamia. Taken from the rear these fortresses did not hold out long.

The Persians lost out just as badly. At Qadasiya in 637 the Arabs' main eastern army won a victory as complete as the battle of the Yarmuk. Seleucia, Ctesiphon and the whole of Iraq were occupied in 638. The subsidiary Arab force occupied Khuzistan.[1]

The next move was a surprise to everyone. Amr ibn al Aasi, commander of the small Arab force in Palestine, decided to abandon a profitless siege of Caesarea (which the Byzantines could supply by sea) and invade Egypt. The caliph reluctantly reinforced him. In 640 Amr defeated the Byzantine army at Heliopolis – the third in the series of desert-edge victories that won the Arabs their empire. Within two more years the whole of Egypt was under the orders of Amr and the rule of the caliph.

Forced out of the Fertile Crescent the Byzantines and Persians found themselves behind the natural defences of the Taurus and Zagros mountains. The Byzantines held the Taurus for more than 400 years.

The Persians, however, collapsed as soon as they were attacked. In 642, the year that Amr completed the conquest of Egypt, the two Arab armies in the east – now based on permanent camps at Kufa and Basra – fought their way on to the Iranian plateau. At the battle of Nehavend they destroyed the main Persian army. All West Persia fell to the invaders.

There was a pause between 644 and 650 while local Persian forces were dealt with, then the conquest of Persia was quickly completed. In 650 the Basra army took Persepolis. The next year it marched northeast to occupy Herat and Merv. It arrived at Merv just too late to capture Yezdegerd III, the last Sassanid king of Persia: the satrap of Merv had had him murdered.

Abu Bekr had died in 634 and the caliph who presided over the great days of Arab expansion was Omar (634–44). A man of ferocious simplicity, Omar was determined to preserve the purity of Islam and of the Arabs. All unbelievers were expelled from Arabia. The Arabs were not allowed to live in the provinces they had conquered: the armies were settled in camps on the edge of the desert. Persia was governed from Kufa and Basra, Syria from Jabiya and Egypt from Fustat (Old Cairo). From each of the camps a desert track led straight back to Medina and the imperious old caliph.

[1] Seleucia, Iraq's biggest city, and Ctesiphon, the administrative capital, lay opposite one another on either side of the Tigris. The Arabs called the two together Medain, 'the twin cities', Medain being the dual of Medina.

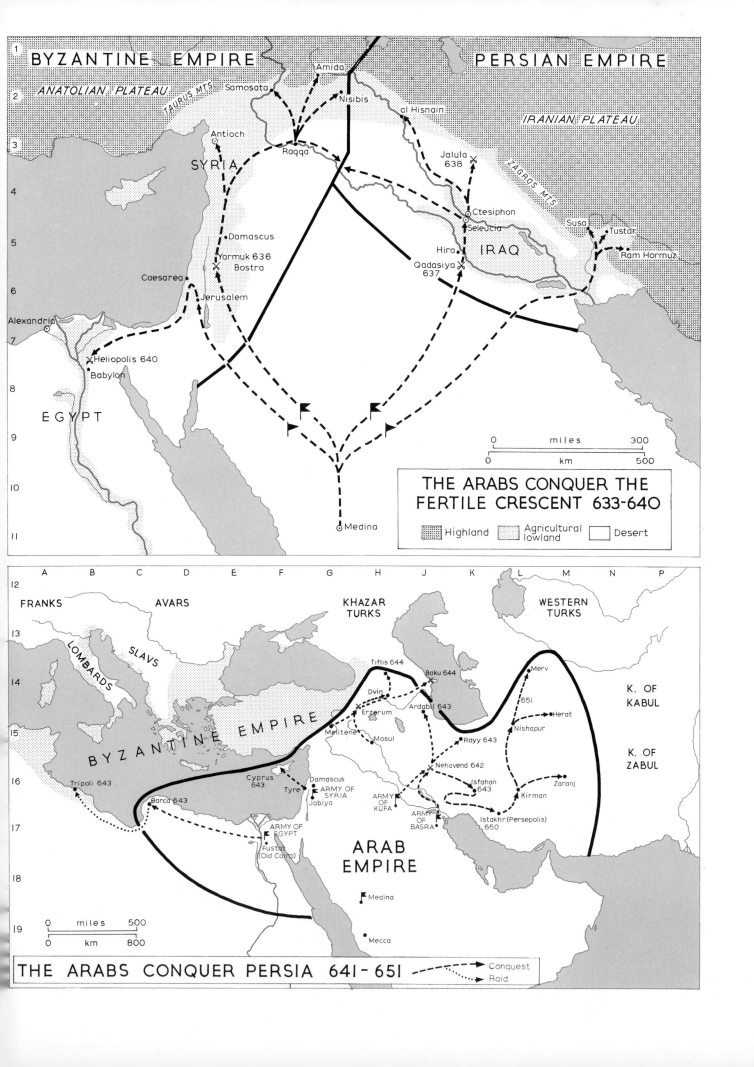

THE ARABS CONQUER THE FERTILE CRESCENT 633-640

BYZANTINE EMPIRE

ANATOLIAN PLATEAU

TAURUS MTS.

PERSIAN EMPIRE

IRANIAN PLATEAU

Amida

Samosata

Nisibis

al Hisnain

ZAGROS MTS

Antioch

SYRIA

Raqqa

Jalula 638

Ctesiphon

Seleucia

Susa

Tustar

Damascus

Hira

IRAQ

Ram Hormuz

Yarmuk 636

Bostra

Qadasiya 637

Caesarea

Jerusalem

Alexandria

Heliopolis 640

Babylon

EGYPT

Medina

	miles		300
0			
0	km		500

THE ARABS CONQUER THE FERTILE CRESCENT 633-640

Highland — Agricultural lowland — Desert

THE ARABS CONQUER PERSIA 641-651

FRANKS

AVARS

KHAZAR TURKS

WESTERN TURKS

LOMBARDS

SLAVS

BYZANTINE EMPIRE

Tiflis 644

Baku 644

Merv

K. OF KABUL

Dvin

Ardabil 643

651

Herat

Erzerum

Nishapur

Melitene

Mosul

Rayy 643

K. OF ZABUL

Tripoli 643

Cyprus 643

Damascus

ARMY OF SYRIA

Jabiya

Nehavend 642

Isfahan 643

Zaranj

Barca 643

Tyre

ARMY OF KUFA

Kirman

ARMY OF EGYPT

ARMY OF BASRA

Istakhr (Persepolis) 650

Fustat (Old Cairo)

ARAB EMPIRE

Medina

Mecca

	miles	500
0		
0	km	800

THE ARABS CONQUER PERSIA 641-651

⤍ Conquest

⋯⋯> Raid

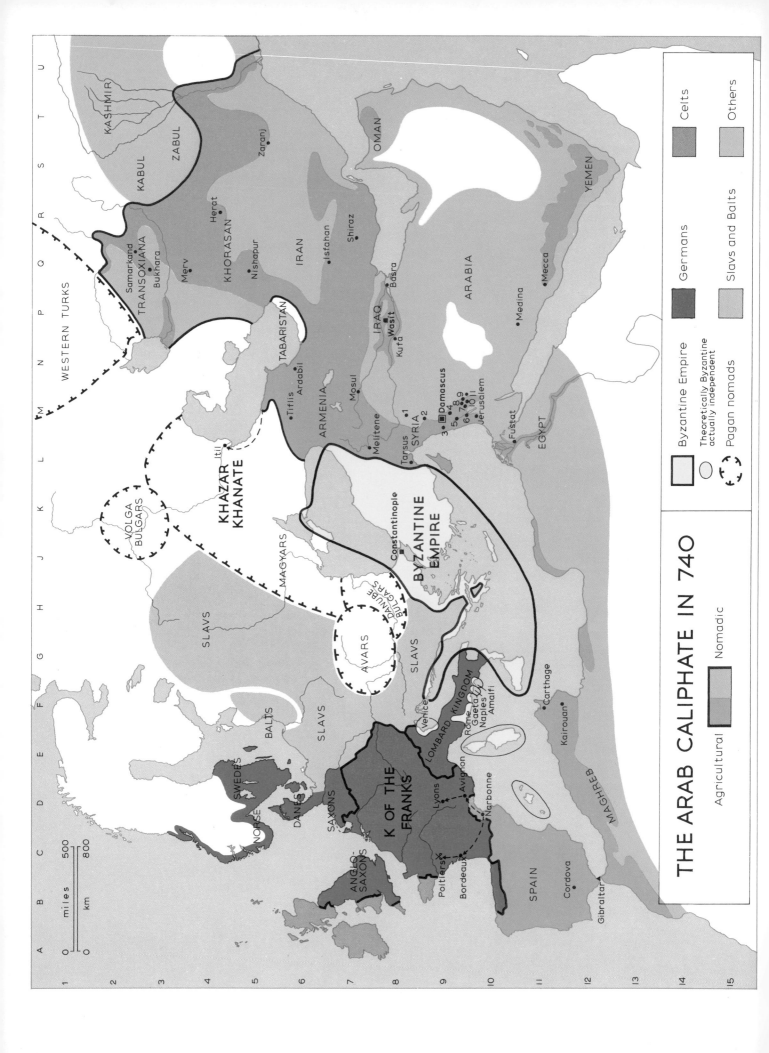

THE ARAB CALIPHATE IN 740

Legend:
- Agricultural
- Nomadic
- Byzantine Empire
- Theoretically Byzantine actually independent
- Pagan nomads
- Celts
- Germans
- Slavs and Balts
- Others

Scale: miles 0 — 500; km 0 — 800

Labels on map:

KASHMIR
KABUL
ZABUL
Zaranj
TRANSOXIANA
Samarkand
Bukhara
Merv
KHORASAN
Herat
Nishapur
IRAN
Isfahan
Shiraz
OMAN
WESTERN TURKS
TABARISTAN
Tiflis
Ardabil
ARMENIA
Mosul
Melitene
Tarsus
SYRIA
Damascus
Jerusalem
IRAQ
Wasit
Kufa
Basra
ARABIA
Mecca
Medina
YEMEN
Fustat
EGYPT
KHAZAR KHANATE
Itil
VOLGA BULGARS
MAGYARS
SLAVS
AVARS
DANUBE BULGARS
BYZANTINE EMPIRE
Constantinople
BALTS
NORSE
SWEDES
DANES
SAXONS
ANGLO-SAXONS
K OF THE FRANKS
Lyons
Poitiers
Bordeaux
Avignon
Narbonne
SPAIN
Cordova
Gibraltar
MAGHREB
Kairouan
Carthage
LOMBARD KINGDOM
Rome
Gaeta
Naples
Amalfi
Venice

The Umayyad Caliphate 661-747

Omar's successor as caliph was Othman (644–55), who belonged to the Umayyad branch of the Quraish.

Othman soon made himself unpopular by giving all the top jobs to his Umayyad relatives. In 655 malcontents from the Fustat, Kufa and Basra armies converged on Medina and murdered him. Ali, son-in-law of the Prophet, was elected caliph in his place.

Not surprisingly Ali made no effort to punish Othman's murderers. Not surprisingly Muawiya, the Umayyad governor of Syria, refused to recognize Ali. Muawiya was a very able man – he had been appointed governor of Syria by Omar and didn't owe anything to Othman's favouritism.

The Bulgars who appear on the map on the Lower Danube and Upper Volga are not a new people; Bulgar is just a new word for Hun. In the 650s the Khazar Turks of the Caucasus defeated the Huns of the Russian steppe and took control of the whole of south Russia. One group of Huns fled to the Danube. The remainder retreated up the Volga. The Khazars forced this second group to recognize their authority.

The Khazar Empire was badly shaken by the Arab invasion of 737 in which their capital, Itil, was sacked. The Bulgars of the Volga regained their independence and most of the Russian steppe passed to the control of the Magyar – a part-Finnish, part-Turkish tribe that had previously been subordinate to the Khazars. The Volga Bulgars, Khazars and Magyars continued to work together and between them these steppe peoples kept the Slav peasants of central Russia firmly under control.

Christendom has lost a lot of ground to Islam. It has also split into two: an Eastern ('Orthodox' or 'Greek') Church obeying the Patriarch of Constantinople and the Western ('Catholic' or 'Latin') Church obeying the Pope in Rome. The cause of the split was the Byzantine emperor's prohibition of religious pictures (icons). He could make the Patriarch of Constantinople obey this order but not the Pope. For in the 720s the Lombards had overrun most of the Exarchate of Ravenna and the bits they didn't conquer – Venice, Rome and Naples were the most important – had become independent states. The Pope still headed all his documents as though Rome was part of the Empire but he ran the Western Church according to his own ideas – which included a soft spot for icons.

The map also shows the sites of the desert palaces of the Umayyad caliphs:

1	Qasr al-Hair ash-Sharqui	7	Mshatta
2	Qasr al-Hair al-Gharbi	8	Hammam as-Sarakh
3	Anjar	9	Quasyr Amra
4	Jabal Says	10	Muwaqqar
5	Minya	11	Qasr at-Tuba
6	Khirbat al-Mafjar		

By 658 he had Ali on the run. When Ali was assassinated in 661 (nothing to do with Muawiya) the Arab Empire fell to Muawiya without much trouble. He had not only become caliph, he made the caliphate hereditary in his family.

Muawiya knew that desert lore was not enough for running an empire. He had administered Syria from Damascus, ignoring Omar's instructions to live in the army camp at Jabiya. Now Damascus was made the capital of the Arab Empire and Arabia once again became a backwater. Muawiya and his immediate successors created a system that kept the empire running.

They also kept it growing, with an impressive list of conquests. Their only failure was an attempt to outflank the Byzantine defence line in the Taurus by mounting a seaborne attack on Constantinople. This failed both times it was tried (670–7 and 716–17) and the Byzantine Empire lived to fight another day. But east and west the armies of Islam continued to advance the frontiers of the caliphate. The campaigns in the east are described on p. 28. Here we concentrate on the victorious campaigns of 699–718 which carried Islam across North Africa and deep into Europe.

The first Arab attempt to conquer North Africa began in 670 when an army from Egypt set up camp at Kairouan in central Tunisia. The Byzantines could only hold out in the seaports but the Berbers gave the Arabs a lot of trouble. At first the Arabs seemed to be getting the upper hand. Then in 683 their commander was killed in an ambush, the Berber tribes rose *en masse* and the Arab army had to be withdrawn to Egypt. Ten years later a new army reoccupied Kairouan, defeated the Berbers and – thanks to an accompanying fleet – captured Carthage and the other Byzantine coastal towns (693–8). The conquest of the Berbers of Tunisia was followed by their conversion to Islam. As the Arab army moved on west into Algeria and Morocco it included Berber contingents.

Normally Arab offensives petered out after a while – even after a major victory. It was the Berber newcomers who prevented this happening in the Maghreb.[1] And it was a Berber column that Tariq, one of the junior commanders, led into Spain. In 711 he landed at the great rock that bears his name (Jebel Tariq 'the mount of Tariq', modern Gibraltar), defeated and killed the Visigothic king and overran most of the kingdom. By 720 all Spain except the cold north coast was part of the caliphate.

One province of the Visigothic kingdom lay over the Pyrenees in southwest France. This was Septimania; its principal town was Narbonne. In 720 the Arabs occupied Narbonne and made it a base for raids into France proper. In 732 they sacked Bordeaux, in 734 Avignon and in 743 Lyons.[2] Would France follow Spain and become another province of the caliphate? If so there would be precious little left of Christendom.

The Umayyad caliphate had now reached a peak of power and glory. Unfortunately the later Umayyad caliphs were not up to their responsibilities: they spent too much time enjoying themselves.

The traditional passions of the Bedouin are hunting and hawking in the desert. The Umayyads made up hunting-parties that were the most magnificent the desert has ever seen – at least until the 20th century and the Cadillac caravans of oil-rich sheiks. At first these hunting-parties used refurbished Roman forts as stop-overs, but soon Umayyad princes were commissioning special hunting-lodges. By the time of the caliph Hisham (724–43) the size of these was spectacular. His successor Walid II started even bigger ones in Transjordan: he spent all his time in the desert and liked to boast that he had never set foot in a town. This was no way to run an empire – within a year Walid had been murdered and the next caliph had to promise that he would live in Damascus.

But by then time was running out for the Umayyads.

---

[1] Maghreb is a catch-all word for Morocco, Algeria and Tunisia.
[2] The force that sacked Bordeaux was cut to pieces later in 732 between Poitiers and Tours. Much has been made of this Frankish victory (won by Charles Martel, see p. 34) but it did not stop the Arabs mounting more raids over the next few years.

21 After Muawiya's death the Umayyads lost control of the Hejaz for a while. As the pilgrimage to Mecca was an essential part of Islam this was a blow to their prestige. In an attempt to get round the problem the Umayyad caliph Abd-al-Malik (685–705) proclaimed Jerusalem an alternative place of pilgrimage.

There were some grounds for the idea: Mohammed had originally ordered his congregations to turn to Jerusalem when they prayed and only substituted Mecca when the local Jews failed to accept Islam. It was also believed by many that on the night of his most perfect vision of God Mohammed had been miraculously transported to Jerusalem and had made the ascent to heaven from the Sacred Rock in the centre of the temple compound (the temple compound was bare, for Herod the Great's temple had gone the way of Solomon's).

Abd-al-Malik had a new temple built to cover the Sacred Rock. It was a much more impressive building than the Meccan Kaaba, but just to make sure he sent a column of soldiers to Mecca and had the Kaaba burnt.

The Dome of the Rock was originally a purely Byzantine building, a grander version of the octagonal Christian Church of the Ascension on the Mount of Olives. As the centuries passed and an Islamic style evolved it got to look more Islamic with every restoration. For example, the tiles that cover the outside date from the time of the Turkish sultan, Suleiman the Magnificent.

In 692 Umayyad soldiers occupied the Hejaz permanently and Jerusalem sank back to third place among Muslim holy cities.

22 The walls of Qasr al-Hair ash-Sharqui, one of the desert palaces built by Caliph Hisham (map 24, no. 1). Qasr means palace, Hair means something between garden and game-reserve and refers to the 850 hectares of surrounding land that were enclosed, stocked and watered so that the caliph could do a little hunting if he fancied it.

MOSQUES AND CHURCHES

The cheapest way of roofing a building is to use wooden rafters and terra cotta tiles. There are various ways of roofing spaces wider than the rafters: the simplest is to place a line of columns carrying an architrave (a horizontal beam) one rafter length from the side wall, roof this section and then repeat the process until the far side is only one rafter length away. This is the system used in most Arab mosques (23). The mosque of Kairouan in Tunisia is a good example (26 *top, left*). The roof is supported on 16 rows of columns, 9 columns to a row. The interior (27 *top, right*) shows the effect – a forest of columns.

This is all very well in brightly lit countries but in Europe it would result in buildings too dark to use. The Romans got over the lighting problem with the basilica design (24). The basilica was usually 4 rafter lengths wide, with 2 rows of columns. The wall-to-column spaces (the aisles) were roofed in the normal way: the column-to-column space (the nave) was two stories high, the columns carrying the walls of the second storey. Windows in the second storey (the clerestory) lit the nave.

The trouble with wooden roofs is that they are always catching fire. If the two storey idea is applied to a round building it is easy to vault the small central space with fireproof brick or concrete (25). This could not be done with a rectangular basilica because the weight of the large vault needed would have been too much for the light clerestory walls.

Nearly all the early Christian churches were basilicas. But in time the Byzantines came to like centrally-planned churches best. All their most famous buildings – S. Vitale and S. Sophia, for example – are developments of this type.[1]

One has to say 'centrally-planned' rather than 'round' because many are octagonal like S. Vitale, or more complex shapes like S. Sophia.

25

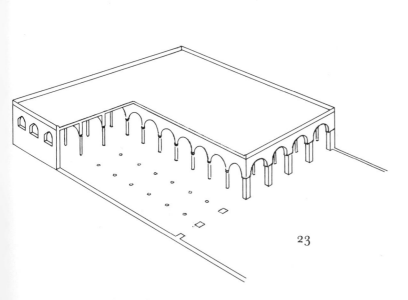

23

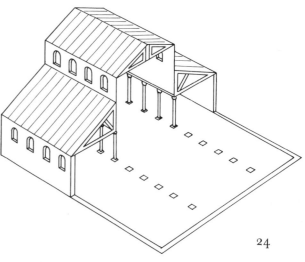

24

The Battle of the River Talas 751

The Sui dynasty that reunited China did not last long. By 618 it had been replaced by the T'ang dynasty – largely as a result of unsuccessful wars with the Koreans and Turks.

The T'ang Empire was durable, lasting for nearly 300 years. For the first half of the period it kept the peace both in China and, rather shakily, in central Asia. T'ang forces occupied the caravan cities of the Takla Makan in 639–48. By playing off one tribe against another the Chinese army commanders were able to keep the east Turks[1] under some sort of control. They even exacted homage from some of the western Turks who now found themselves squeezed between the Chinese and the armies of the Arab caliphate.

At the beginning of the 8th century the caliphate began its second period of expansion. One Arab army marched across south Persia into India in 712. In two campaigns this force conquered the Lower Indus region. The army in northeast Persia (Khorasan) took Balkh in 705, and then moved across the Oxus to Bokhara (709) and Samarkand (712).

These cities were under the rule of the western Turks. Their inhabitants appealed to the Turks for protection and they in turn appealed to China for help. The Chinese governor of An-si[2] marched through the Tien Shan (Celestial Mountains), collected his Turkish allies and met the Arabs and *their* Turkish allies on the banks of the River Talas. He was completely defeated. Over the next few years Chinese power in central Asia collapsed.

The battle of the River Talas has been called one of the decisive battles of history, deciding the struggle between China and Islam in favour of Islam. But that is making far too much of it. The Chinese defeat was in an area where they never had any real control. The area itself did not pass into Arab hands, it remained Turkish. The collapse of Chinese power in central Asia was more the result of the bitter civil war at home after An Lu-shan's revolt (see p. 30) than the battle of the River Talas. In reality this was just a battle between two sets of Turks with Arab and Chinese allies and it marked nothing except the victory of one Turkish clan over another. What the Chinese held then is still a Chinese province today (known as Sinkiang) and though it is true that the inhabitants of Sinkiang are Moslem the spread of Islam into central Asia was by conversion not by conquest.

[1] The Turkish khanate had split in 581.
[2] An-si means 'the pacified west' just as An-nan (the protectorate established by the Chinese over north Vietnam) means 'the pacified south'. The Chinese also referred to An-si as 'the four garrisons' after the four major oasis-cities of the Tarim Basin – Kutcha, Kashgar, Karachahr and Khotan.

28 Bronze Buddha from Horyuji. Cast by Tori Busshi in 623

BUDDHISM IN JAPAN AND INDONESIA

At the end of the 6th century the Japanese became aware of China. The scale and style of Chinese civilization made the Japanese feel like barbarians, which indeed they were. They immediately decided they were going to catch up. In little more than a generation Japan was remade in the Chinese image and the Japanese emperor had a court and a capital (the entirely new city of Nara) rivalling anything in China.

Part of this modernization programme was the adoption of Buddhism. Monasteries were built in great numbers. The one shown in illustration 29 (*opposite, left*) is Horyuji, near Nara, built *c.* 680. All the buildings are wooden and it is a tribute to the care the Japanese have always taken of them that they are still standing: they are in fact the oldest wooden buildings in the world.

The centre of the monastery is the courtyard which is entered by the gatehouse on the near left side. In the court are a five-storey pagoda and a two-storey hall containing statues of the Buddha. Behind them is the monk's lecture hall and on either side of this are a library (far corner) and a bell house (right-hand corner).

The pagoda was one type of shrine evolved by the Buddhists: another was the stupa. The stupa, originally a simple mound to mark a holy spot, was later elaborated in a way that is best shown at Borobodur – the sole surviving monument of the Indonesian kings of Sri Vijaya.

Borobodur (30 *opposite, right*) is a hill that has been cased in to make a low-profile step pyramid. Sunk into the rim of each of its five steps is a corridor, the walls of which are lined with reliefs illustrating the Buddha's life. Each stage up, the Buddha becomes less involved with the things of this world and more serenely part of the next. The pilgrim who followed all five corridors round had re-enacted the Buddha's own process of enlightenment (and walked about 5 km). He then emerged on a platform open to the sky – he had left the earth behind. Facing him rose three platforms – circular because this is the shape of the Buddhist heaven. On them were 72 images of Buddha housed in fretwork shrines (a mortal can only half understand the Buddha). In the centre of the topmost platform was a huge solid-walled shrine concealing the final image that is beyond human understanding.

Borobodur is not a building in the usual sense – it is a model of the universe as conceived by Buddhists and a guide to how to attain 'enlightenment'.

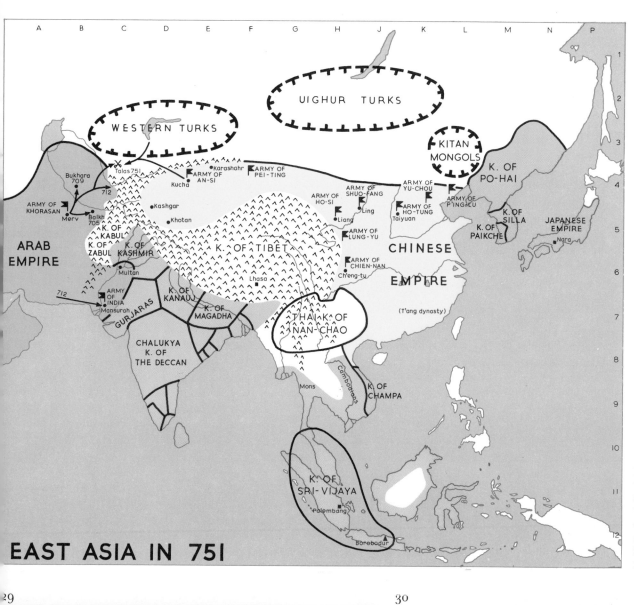

EAST ASIA IN 751

WESTERN TURKS

UIGHUR TURKS

KITAN MONGOLS

ARAB EMPIRE

Bukhara 709
Talas 751
ARMY OF KHORASAN
Merv
Balkh 705
712
Kucha
Kashgar
Khotan
K. OF KABUL
K. OF ZABUL
K. OF KASHMIR
Multan
712
ARMY OF INDIA
Mansurah
GURJARAS
K. OF KANAUJ
K. OF MAGADHA
CHALUKYA K. OF THE DECCAN
Karashahr
ARMY OF AN-SI
ARMY OF PEI-TING
ARMY OF HO-SI
ARMY OF SHUO-FANG
Liang
Ling
ARMY OF LUNG-YU
ARMY OF CHIEN-NAN
Ch'eng-tu
Lhasa
K. OF TIBET
THA. K. OF NAN-CHAO
Mons
Cambodians
K. OF CHAMPA
ARMY OF YU-CHOU
ARMY OF HO-TUNG
Taiyuan
ARMY OF P'ING-LU
CHINESE EMPIRE
(T'ang dynasty)
K. OF PO-HAI
K. OF SILLA
K. OF PAIKCHE
JAPANESE EMPIRE
Nara
K. OF SRI-VIJAYA
Palembang
Borobudur

In those cases where the Chinese armies' garrison towns are not given on the map the name of the town is the same as the name of the army.

29   30

China under the Sui and T'ang Dynasties 580-900

31 Turkish cavalry-man

The China of the Sui and T'ang emperors still bore the imprint of the steppe peoples. The Yellow River valley – the heartland of China – had been dominated by the nomads for so long that the local aristocracy was as much Turkish as Chinese. For that matter so were the emperors. Nevertheless, the new rulers were entirely Chinese in spirit. Under their command China resumed the social development that the first nomad dynasties had interrupted.

For the educated Chinese there was only one system of government, the civil service system idealized by Confucius. The officials were to be carefully chosen for their intelligence, hard work and honesty. Government academies were to train suitable candidates regardless of birth and to weed them out by a series of examinations.

This was a remarkable ideal to hold at a time when the rest of the world was run by tribal chiefs or feudal lords and when even literate aristocrats saw clerks as a very low form of life. Even more remarkable the Confucians managed to create a service that was pretty much like their ideal. They never got rid of the aristocratic party but they controlled day-to-day administration. And in the first half of the Sui-T'ang period they kept the army firmly in place.

It was one thing to bring justice to the 2000 *hsien* (counties) of rural China. It was another to keep the soldiers happy. China did not have a money economy. Taxes were paid in kind, grain and clothing being the most important categories. It was impossibly slow and wasteful to transport these goods by land: they had to go by river or canal. Now the armies, for strategic reasons, had to be stationed in the north, but if they could only draw supplies from the Yellow River valley China was no stronger for being united.

The second Sui emperor, Yang Ti, saw that the answer was a canal linking the Yangtze with the Yellow River. By his ruthless use of forced labour – $5\frac{1}{2}$ million men are said to have been employed, of whom 2 million were 'lost' – he completed the canal in four years. Now the surplus wheat and rice of the Yangtze could be brought to Lo-yang and sent down the Yellow River to the armies manning the Great Wall.[1]

Thanks to their well-supplied army the early T'ang were able to keep a firm grip on Inner Mongolia. Unfortunately this involved them in war with the Koreans. This was long drawn out and costly. In the end T'ang generals destroyed the North Korean kingdom of Koguryo and re-duced the South Korean kingdom of Silla to obedience (668), but by then the Chinese exchequer was complaining that the burden of the fighting was too much for the country. The victorious armies were withdrawn: North Korea being abandoned to the Po-hai and much of the Inner Mongolian steppe to the Kitan Mongols. Immediately the Kitan turned on their Chinese masters. Instead of bringing peace the policy of cost-cutting brought the war to China's doorstep.

The armies of the early T'ang emperors were conscripted from the Chinese peasantry. But peasants make reluctant soldiers and, as the memory of conquering Turks faded, the T'ang used more and more nomad mercenaries. By the time of the battle of the River Talas the armies were mostly Turkish.

This was also true of the generals. By 751 only one of the nine armies (the one in Chien-nan, which was the least important) had a native Chinese in command. Worse still An Lu-shan, the Turkish general in charge of the war against the Kitan Mongols, was soon allowed to assume command of all three armies in the northeast.

This was asking for trouble. In 756 An Lu-shan fell out with the government, marched west, sacked both imperial capitals and proclaimed himself emperor. The T'ang managed to save themselves by calling in the Uighur Turks who defeated An Lu-shan.

But the empire was never the same again. Indeed, with Turks and Tibetans loose in the north and every general playing his own hand, things at first looked absolutely hopeless.

The T'ang administrators did manage to get back some sort of control by the end of the 8th century. They did this partly by playing off one general against another, partly by creating more army commands so that no one general could become too powerful. By 810 there were thirty small armies where less than a century before there had been seven big ones.[2] The T'ang court was able to control about half these commands, the rest were really independent little states run by what the Chinese call 'war lords'.

By the 9th century the T'ang administration was only a shadow of its former self but it had to face a new problem: peasant risings. These were caused by the government's inability to protect the peasantry from the war lords. The administration made a valiant effort to cope with the risings and in 878 T'ang generals succeeded in chasing the greatest of the peasant leaders, Huang Ch'ao

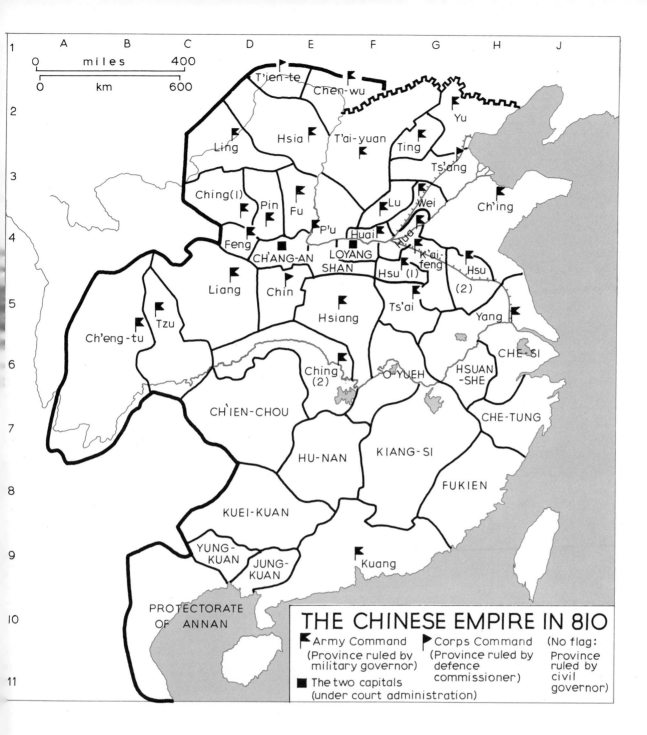

THE CHINESE EMPIRE IN 810

Army Command
(Province ruled by
military governor)

Corps Command
(Province ruled by
defence
commissioner)

(No flag:
Province
ruled by
civil
governor)

The two capitals
(under court administration)

way from the Yellow River. Huang Ch'ao made a long march to the south, took Canton and built up his forces again. Then in 880 he marched back to the north, the imperial army melting away before him.

For the last time the T'ang dynasty saved itself by calling in the Turks of the steppe. But on this occasion they gained very little time. In 907 the military governor of K'aifeng deposed the T'ang emperor and founded a new dynasty – the first of five that were to rule the Yellow River valley in quick sequence. Meanwhile the south had split up into half a dozen separate kingdoms.

The long drawn-out death agony of the T'ang

Empire had never dimmed its lustre in Chinese eyes. The T'ang did, after all, rule more of Asia for a longer time than any other dynasty that can reasonably be called Chinese. And the styles defined by the scholars, artists and craftsmen of the T'ang court dominated Chinese culture from then until modern times. It was China's classic age.

[1] Yangtze grain was also used to support the imperial court. It was expensive to get it to Chang-an because it had to be hauled round the San-men rapids by ox-cart. So in really bad years the court moved to Lo-yang.

[2] There are nine Chinese armies on map 29 but by 810 the empire no longer included the An-si and Pei-t'ing commands.

The Kingdom of the Franks 511-741

32 Frankish cavalry-man

Of all the German tribes who established themselves in the shell of the Western Roman Empire only one was really successful. As Ostrogoths, Vandals, Suevi and Visigoths disappeared from the map it was the Franks who thrived and expanded.

They conquered the Thuringians, Gascons and Burgundians. When Justinian attacked the Ostrogoths they seized Ostrogothic Switzerland and southern France. When the Ostrogothic kingdom finally collapsed they took over Bavaria. Frankish kings were to rule this much or more of Europe for the next 400 years.

Why did the Franks succeed where the other Germans failed? Partly because, unlike the Vandals and Visigoths, their slice of the Roman Empire bordered on Germany. Their success did not lead to them getting spread too thinly, it simply attracted more Germans to the Frankish banner. Another reason is that under Clovis, the Franks had become Catholics. The Goths, Vandals and Burgundians were Arian Christians, which caused friction between them and their Catholic subjects. The Catholics in Visigothic Gaul welcomed Clovis as a liberator.

Finally, the Franks made little effort to maintain the outdated Roman system of government. Where Theodoric the Ostrogoth and other German kings levied the old taxes, tried to revive the decaying cities and talked of restoring the Roman Empire, the Franks let the whole machine run down. The economic trends we have noted in the later Western Empire – the decline of the towns, the diminishing use of money – were allowed to proceed to completion. By the end of the 7th century there were no towns and no taxes in the Frankish kingdom. It was a rural society held together purely by the loyalty of the Franks to their king.

This loyalty must have been strong – the kingdom survived many attempts to divide it. Clovis and the kings who followed him regarded the kingdom as a private estate: however many sons there were, each got his share. But so many sons died without heirs that the kingdom kept coming together again. This sounds like luck but if there

had been any backing for a real breakaway there were plenty of opportunities. The Franks must have had a very strong sense of unity.

Clovis, who died in 511, had four sons. Each got a part of the original kingdom and a part of the new lands conquered by their father. Their kingdoms looked like this.

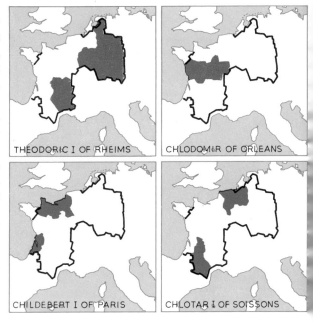

By 558 the youngest son, Chlotar 1, had inherited the shares of the other three. Like Clovis he had four sons and a new division took place on his death.

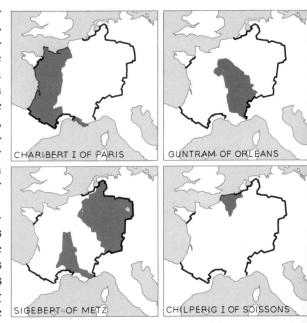

32

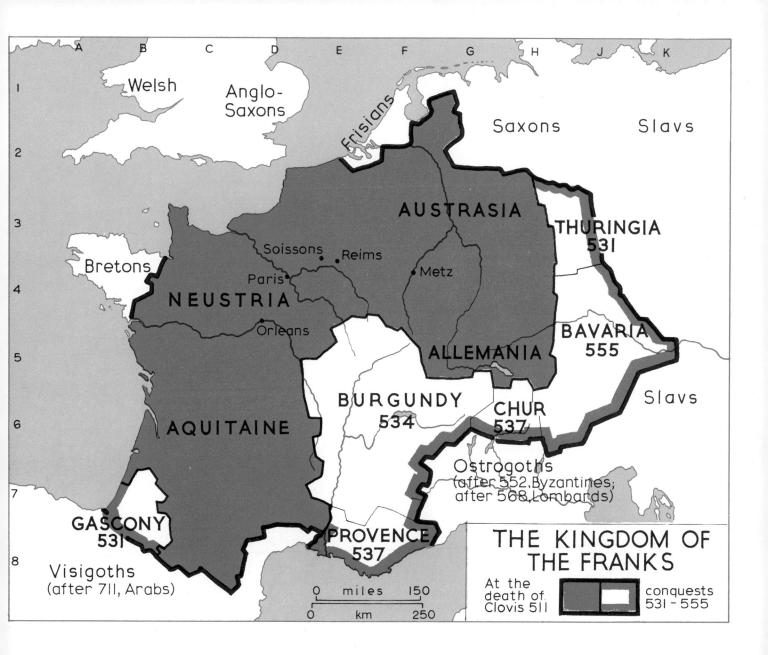

THE KINGDOM OF
THE FRANKS

At the
death of
Clovis 511 / conquests
531 - 555

Welsh

Anglo-
Saxons

Frisians

Saxons   Slavs

AUSTRASIA

THURINGIA
531

Soissons   Reims

Bretons

Paris

NEUSTRIA

Metz

BAVARIA
555

Orleans

ALLEMANIA

Slavs

BURGUNDY
534

CHUR
537

AQUITAINE

Ostrogoths
(after 552,Byzantines;
after 568,Lombards)

GASCONY
531

PROVENCE
537

Visigoths
(after 711, Arabs)

0   miles   150
0   km   250

By 613 all these kingdoms were under the rule of
Chlotar II, the sole surviving grandson of Chlotar I.
Ten years later he gave the 'eastern land'
Austrasia to his son Dagobert, keeping the 'new
land' Neustria for himself.
This became the usual division thereafter.

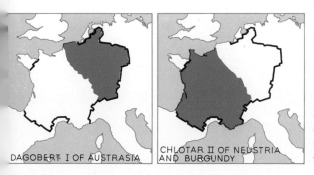

DAGOBERT I OF AUSTRASIA

CHLOTAR II OF NEUSTRIA
AND BURGUNDY

After Dagobert (629–39) none of the descendants of Clovis had any real power. Indeed there
seems to have been something genetically wrong
with them, for they mostly died in their teens.
Effective power fell into the hands of the 'mayors
of the palace'. It was Pepin, mayor of the palace
in Austrasia, who eventually reunited the kingdom (687). In effect Pepin founded a new
dynasty though it was a long while before any of
his descendants actually sat on the throne. His son
Charles Martel – the man who beat the Arabs at
Poitiers – ran the whole Frankish kingdom from
719 to 741 but even he did not feel it would be
right to take the crown. Until his last few years he
always ruled through puppet kings of the line of
Clovis, and when this line ended he didn't take
the throne himself – he simply left it vacant.

33

Charlemagne 768-814

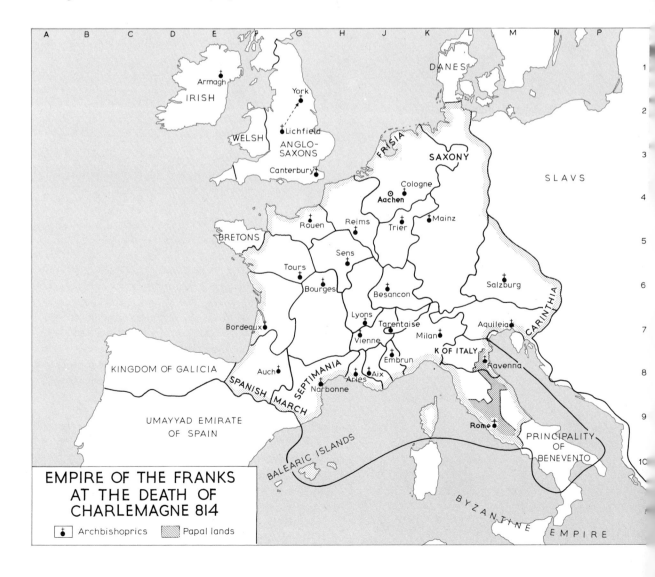

33 Charlemagne dressed as a Roman emperor

By the middle of the 8th century the Byzantine forces in north Italy had become so weak that the Lombards were able to move in on the Exarchate of Ravenna.

The Pope had no wish for a Lombard king as overlord. He appealed to the Franks to save him, and though his first appeal (to Charles Martel in 739) fell on deaf ears the next (to Charles' son and successor Pepin the Short) was more successful. On his part the Pope gave permission for Pepin to take the Frankish throne and make himself ruler in name as well as fact (751). In return Pepin told the Lombards to lay off Rome and, when they failed to do so, crossed the Alps and brought them to heel. Pepin also conquered Septimania, driving the Arabs back into Spain. It was a vigorous, if barbaric, kingdom that he passed on to his son Charles.[1]

Charles has gone down into history as Charlemagne – Charles the Great (*magnus* is the Latin for 'great'). This is mainly because he was a determined and successful soldier. He went campaigning most years of his long reign. When the Lombards caused trouble again he annexed their kingdom. He also conquered the Saxons, the last free tribe of Germany, destroyed the Avar kingdom in Hungary and established supremacy of a sort over the Slav tribes along the whole length of

Though the administrative system of Roman Gaul faded away its outline was preserved by the Catholic church. Its bishoprics are the *civitates* – the 'cities' – into which the Empire had been divided: its parishes are the *pagi*, the rural districts which made up the territory of each 'city'. And its archbishoprics – the divisions shown on the map – are the old Roman provinces.

Note that although Christianity had advanced into Germany there were still no archbishoprics in this part of Charlemagne's empire. As a result the archbishoprics on the Rhine became the possessors of vast estates. The archbishop of Mainz was one of the most powerful men in the Empire.

EMPIRE OF THE FRANKS AT THE DEATH OF CHARLEMAGNE 814

Archbishoprics   Papal lands

34 Charles the Bald

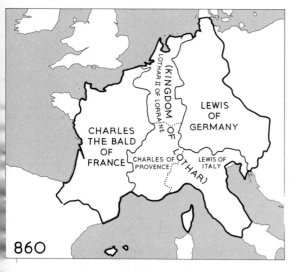

860

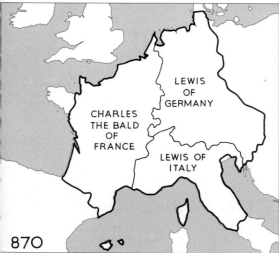

870

900

his east frontier. His only failure was his attack on the Moslems of Spain: all he acquired there was an unimportant strip of land along the south side of the Pyrenees.

By the middle of his reign Charlemagne had brought almost the whole of western Christendom into the kingdom of the Franks.[2] People were impressed and the Pope – saved from the Lombards and enriched by the gift of the old Byzantine territory in north Italy – was particularly so. In the year 800 when Charlemagne was attending mass at St Peter's in Rome the Pope sprung a surprise. He placed a crown on Charlemagne's head and proclaimed the Roman Empire of the west restored with Charlemagne as its emperor. Charles, though somewhat alarmed, went along with the idea. In the end even the Byzantine emperor recognized his title.

Really the whole thing was nonsense. Three strong kings in succession – Charles Martel, Pepin the Short and now Charlemagne – had made the Frankish kingdom appear a lot more impressive than it really was. It functioned because when Charles called the warrior barons to the 'Field of May', the annual muster of the army, they came. If under a weak successor they did not, the new empire would fall apart. The administration that could keep an empire going through a bad period was entirely lacking.

Charlemagne intended to follow Frankish custom and divide his empire between his sons. But only one, Louis the Pious, survived him. So the Empire remained united till Louis' death in 840. Louis did try to break with tradition and leave the whole empire to his oldest son, Lothar. But Lothar's brothers Charles and Lewis forced him to give them independent kingdoms. Lothar soon died, leaving three sons to divide up his share (top map).

By 870 two of the sons of Lothar, Lothar I of Lorraine and Charles of Provence, were dead and Charles the Bald and Lewis the German had divided their possessions between them (middle map). The empire had now split up into units roughly corresponding to France, Germany and Italy. These were natural divisions both in terms of geography and peoples – the Franks of France were now French-speaking, the Frankish nobility of Italy Italian-speaking.[3]

But Charlemagne's descendants were now dying faster than they were multiplying so the empire did come together again, in 884. Then in 887–8 it split up for good. Two barons fought each other for the crown of Italy, two others carved out little kingdoms for themselves in Burgundy and Provence, while a fifth became king of France. In theory they all acknowledged the king of Germany, the only adult member of the House of Charlemagne left, as superior. In practice they were independent monarchs. The empire of Charlemagne had ceased to exist.

[1] Pepin left part of his kingdom to his other son Carloman but he outlived his father by only three years.
[2] Excepting the British Isles, the Bretons, the Spanish kingdom of Asturias and the Lombard principality of Benevento in south Italy.
[3] Frankish was a German language but French, like Italian, had evolved from the Latin spoken in these ex-provinces of the Roman Empire.

35

Britain becomes England
400-800

The Roman province of Britain at first had only one frontier – the wall that divided it from unconquered Scotland (Pict-land as it was then). In the 4th century a second defence system was set up: a chain of forts on the east coast whose commander was known as the Count of the Saxon Shore. Obviously by this time the Saxons of northwest Germany had started to attack Britain.

Like all the German attacks on the empire the motive was more to seize land than plunder. Whether the attackers were defeated or not didn't make much difference – because the Romans were short of manpower they used to settle defeated tribes on land inside the empire. As a result Britain probably had quite a large German population along its east coast by the time the Romans left.

For thirty or forty years after the Roman soldiers were called home by Stilicho (see p. 8) British and Germans seem to have lived side by side happily enough. Then the British brought in more Germans as mercenaries to fight the Picts. These mercenaries soon set up on their own. Too late the British woke up to the fact that their eastern seaboard was in the hands of an alien people. Germans started to pour in from the other side of the North Sea and move up the rivers into the heart of the country. In the last half of the 5th century the British lost the whole of the southwest to a wave of German immigrants.

The Germans who turned Britain into England were the Saxons, the Angles (who gave the country its new name of Angle-land) and the Jutes. There is no dispute as to where the Angles and Saxons came from but there has been a lot of argument about the Jutes. People used to think that they came from Jutland at the north end of the Danish peninsula. Now it is generally agreed that they were one of the Frisian tribes who lived in the Low Countries.

The Jutes settled Kent and the Isle of Wight. The Saxons occupied the Thames valley and divided into west, middle, south and east groups (hence Wessex, Middlesex, Sussex and Essex). The Angles split into middle, east and north groups (only East Anglia survives in English geography).

Around 490, after a generation of defeats, the British rallied and beat back a West Saxon thrust to the Severn.[1] After this there was peace in the south for fifty years. Then the advance began again. The second time the West Saxons reached the Severn they won the resulting battle (at Dyrham, 577). The Northumbrian (north-of-the-Humber) Angles won a matching victory over the British of the northwest (at Chester, 616) and conquered the whole north.

As a result of these two battles the British kingdoms in Wales were cut off from those in the north (the kingdom of Strathclyde) and south (the kingdom of Devon). This put an end to any hope of a British comeback: indeed the term British disappears and from now on the surviving British are referred to as Welsh.

There were originally more than a dozen Anglo-Saxon kingdoms. One king was usually recognized as 'Bretwalda' – 'Britain-ruler' – by the others but at first the title simply meant that he was agreed to be the most powerful king in the country. It did not give him any extra power nor was it hereditary. In the 670s the kings of Mercia, the Anglian kingdom of the Midlands, gained the title and put a lot more meaning into it. They annexed the small kingdoms on their borders – Magon (Hereford), Hwicce (Worcester), Middlesex (which included Surrey, its south region), the kingdom of the Middle Angles and Lindsay (Lincoln). The kingdoms that remained free in theory lost a lot of their independence. In the days of Offa, king of Mercia from 757 to 796, every ruler south of the Humber had to get his approval for any important act.

Like the early Chinese the Anglo-Saxons often marked important boundaries with earth walls. King Offa built one along the whole of the Welsh frontier. Whether he meant it to or not this marked the end of the Anglo-Saxon advance. Eighty per cent of the inhabitants of Britain (about a million altogether) were now either English or living under English control.[2]

[1] The British victory occurred at 'the siege of Mount Badon' of which nothing is known for sure, not even the site. We do know that it was the only battle in which the British had anything to crow about – and that they certainly *did* crow. Within a few generations they had come to believe that this was only one in a string of victories won by a hero named Arthur. And after that the stories got really wild. Arthur was supposed to have overcome the Anglo-Saxons completely, made himself king of all Britain and then conquered much of western Europe.

The legend of King Arthur was carried to France by refugees who fled from Devon to the Brest peninsula (hence 'Brittany'). French poets are responsible for many of the finer flourishes, including the Round Table.

[2] The West Saxons had conquered the heart of the kingdom of Devon by 720 but they did not completely occupy Cornwall till 838. Eastward they had conquered the Jutes of the Isle of Wight and the nearby mainland in 685.

The Scots who appear on map B were Ulstermen who occupied the Argyll region in the 5th century and set up an independent kingdom of their own in the 6th.

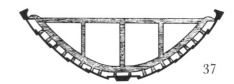

36 The Nydam ship. This is the sort of boat that the Anglo-Saxons used to get to Britain. It is 23 m long and has places for 14 oarsmen a side. There is no mast: it is a rowing-boat pure and simple.

The cross section (37) shows how the hull is built of over-lapping planks. Ships constructed in this way are said to be 'clinker-built'. The system is characteristic of North Sea craft. Also typical is the single steering oar and the symmetrically sharp bow and stern. Mediterranean vessels had a rounded stern and a steering oar on each side of it.

The Nydam ship does not look up to much but a dozen of them doing a round trip a year could move 100,000 people in a century. As the migration to Britain went on for about three centuries (350–650) this rate, plus some natural increase by the settlers, is quite enough to account for the creation of an English-speaking England.

The Nydam ship was found preserved in a bog in Schleswig (the part of the Danish peninsula in which the Angles lived) in 1863.

A THE ANGLO-SAXONS SETTLE IN BRITAIN — Frontiers of 550

B ENGLAND UNDER KING OFFA OF MERCIA — Frontiers of 796

38 Swedish sailing-
ship

Charlemagne's conquest of Saxony brought the empire's frontier to the base of the Danish peninsula. The Franks had gained a new set of neighbours, the Scandinavians. No one thought much of this: Scandinavia was a backwater and seemed likely to remain so.

Denmark at this time was bigger than it is today. The Danes had absorbed the Angles of the south half of the peninsula; they also held the south part of Sweden. A population of nearly half a million made them the most important of the Scandinavian peoples.

North of the Danes were the Norwegians or Norse. About 100,000 of them lived on the shores of the Vik, facing Denmark. As many again lived in settlements scattered along the Atlantic coastline as far north as Trondheim.

The third group, the Swedes, lived on the Baltic

[1] The population of Scandinavia lived entirely in the south half of the peninsula. North Scandinavia was an empty Ice Age world. Its only inhabitants were a few thousand Lapps herding reindeer on the Atlantic side of the mountains and a few thousand Finns fishing the rivers on the Baltic side.

side of Scandinavia round the inlet that is the present-day Lake Malar. Originally there had been a tribe of Goths between the Swedes and the Danes. This was the parent tribe of the Goths who had colonized east Germany, migrated to south Russia and then played such an important part in the fall of the Western Roman Empire. Towards the end of the 6th century these Goths of Scandinavia had been conquered by the Swedes. The name Gothland remained in use (as it still does) but the people were absorbed. They brought Swedish numbers up to a figure near the Danish.[1]

In Charlemagne's time the Swedes were already united under one king. So were the Danes from time to time, though usually they were quarrelling about who the king was. The Norse had not reached the stage of thinking of themselves as one people: a Norseman, if asked his nationality,

SCANDINAVIA 800

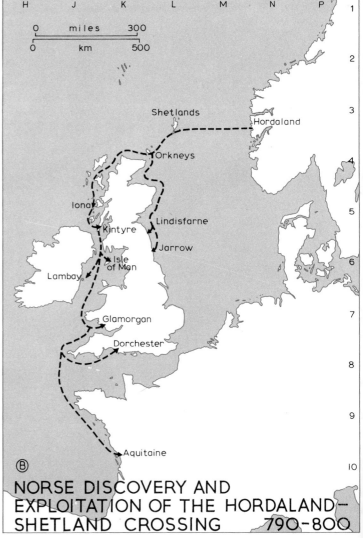

NORSE DISCOVERY AND EXPLOITATION OF THE HORDALAND—SHETLAND CROSSING 790-800

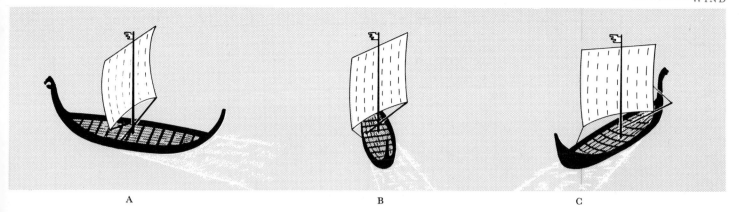

A   B   C

would think of his home province and say he was a Hordalander or a Trondheimer or whatever.

As we have said the rest of Europe was not very interested in Scandinavia, which seemed an unchanging backwater, pagan and poverty-stricken. But in the 8th century the Scandinavians learnt to make something that no one else could – a really efficient sailing-ship.

It is easy enough to build a sailing-ship that can run before the wind. For thousands of years there had been sailing-ships of this sort in the Mediterranean and elsewhere. In most cases their captains sailed by day and kept the shore in sight so they could use their oars to pull in if the wind turned against them. On a few routes, such as the Red Sea/India and India/Malaya sections of the Spice Route, seamen had learnt to use the monsoon winds to cut across the open sea (see p. 5). But no one tried this sort of thing unless he was sure the wind would hold throughout the voyage and there were few places and times one could be sure of that.

Sailing-ships of this type were not much use in the tricky winds of the north. That is why the early Scandinavians used rowing-boats like the Nydam ship. Then the Norse solved the problem of how to make use of variable winds. The new boats could sail across the wind: they could even sail into it (see the diagram above).

Around 790 the Norse of Hordaland, trying out their new sailing-ships, discovered the Shetland Islands and the nearby Orkneys. From there they made a series of voyages to the south. In 793 they plundered the monastery of Lindisfarne on the northeast coast of England. The next year they returned and sacked the monastery at Jarrow. This time they met rather stiffer opposition so they made their next voyages down the west side of England where sailing conditions too were easier. Soon they had explored the whole coastline from the Hebrides to Cornwall. In 799 Norse ships even reached the Bay of Biscay.

You can get some idea of how much better the new boats were than the old if you compare map B on the opposite page with map A on p. 37. The Anglo-Saxons' cautious shuttle along the Frisian coast is quite outclassed by the Norse exploration. And these voyages were only the first of many.

39 If you look at a ship with its sails spread to catch the wind you usually think of the sail as a bag holding the wind and receiving its thrust. The seamen of the ancient world seem to have thought of sails in this way. But the wind is not a solid object giving a direct thrust, it is a flow of particles. What the sail does is deflect these and the way it works is just the same as an aeroplane's wing. That is why the ship sailing across the wind (B) is able to do so: the sail functions as a vertical aerofoil turning the air stream backwards and generating forward thrust. If the sail is put in a 'fore and aft' position (C) it will even drive the boat *into* the wind. This trick requires special spars and rigging, a good rudder and a strong keel as well, but we know that the Norse ships had all these and modern reconstructions have shown that they could do it.

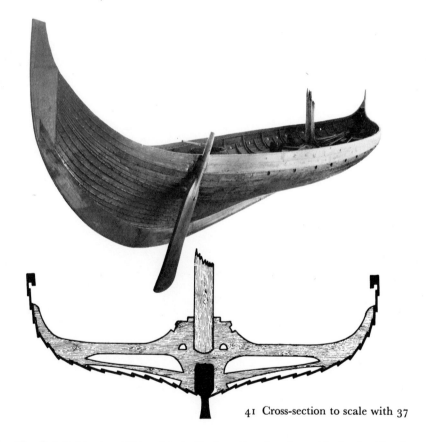

41 Cross-section to scale with 37

40 The Gokstad boat, a Viking ship built about 875. Leaving aside the fact that it is really a sailing vessel and considering it just as a rowing-boat, the advances over the Nydam ship are striking. The hull is more carefully built (using 16 planks each side to the Nydam ship's 5), it is a more sophisticated shape (nearly twice as wide for the same length), and whereas the oarsmen in the Nydam ship simply put their oars over the side, in the Gokstad ship they ran them out through portholes which could be closed when not in use.

However the essential difference between the Nydam and Gokstad ships is that the latter is a sailing vessel. This means it has not only a mast but also interior and exterior keels. The interior keel – a single oak timber running the length of the ship – gives the vessel the strength to stand up to Atlantic gales. The exterior keel gives it enough grip in the water to sail against the wind.

The Vikings 800-950

42 Viking warriors

Norse stories of easy spoils to the west took a long time to reach Denmark. It was only in the 830s that the Danes began to join in. Then life immediately became very precarious for people living beside the English Channel. And as the Danes and Norse learnt the way up the big rivers it became dangerous for people inland, too. In the second half of the 9th century most of west Europe lived in dread of a raid by 'Vikings'.

Viking means any Scandinavian raider. Chroniclers at the time had great difficulty distinguishing between Norse and Danes and the word does for both. Nowadays we have a fairly clear picture of who was responsible for what but we still call the period the Viking Age.[1]

From the European point of view the worst part of the Viking Age began in the 850s when the raiders stopped going home for the winter and began to camp instead at the mouths of the rivers that were their highroads. Viking forces were not very large, the fleets numbered their boats in tens and the raiding parties were rarely as much as 1000 strong. But even so the best organized countries had great difficulty coping. The Vikings could cut up anything short of a full army, and at that time it was a slow business getting an army together – usually far too slow to catch any Vikings.

The biggest Danish venture was the landing of the 'Great Army' on the east coast of England in 866. All the Anglo-Saxon kingdoms crumbled before it as it left its boats behind, marched up to Northumbria then down again to the Midlands. Alfred the Great managed to hold the kingdom of Wessex together and in 878 a frontier was fixed by treaty between Wessex and Danish England.

Many Danes settled in this half of England which came to be called the Danelaw, but leaving Wessex unconquered eventually cost them their freedom. By 900 the men of Wessex were on the offensive: by 954 they had conquered the Danelaw and the kings of Wessex had become the kings of England. By then the Irish too had expelled the Norse and Danes who had terrorized them for three generations.

On the continent the raids also died away in the early 10th century. In 911 the French king gave the Viking Rollo the lands at the mouth of the Seine on condition he kept his fellow Vikings from attacking the kingdom. It seems to have worked. Rollo built up his fief into the Duchy of Normandy, 'land of the Northmen'. Many Vikings settled there and gave up their roving ways. Indeed it was the settlements in the Danelaw, Normandy and other areas that brought the Viking attacks to an end. Now the landless sons had found farms – or graves – abroad.

[1] We have seen that Oslofiord was called the Vik. Any creek or inlet could be called a vik, so the word Viking means something like 'men of the waterways'.

43 Reconstruction drawing
of the Gokstad ship

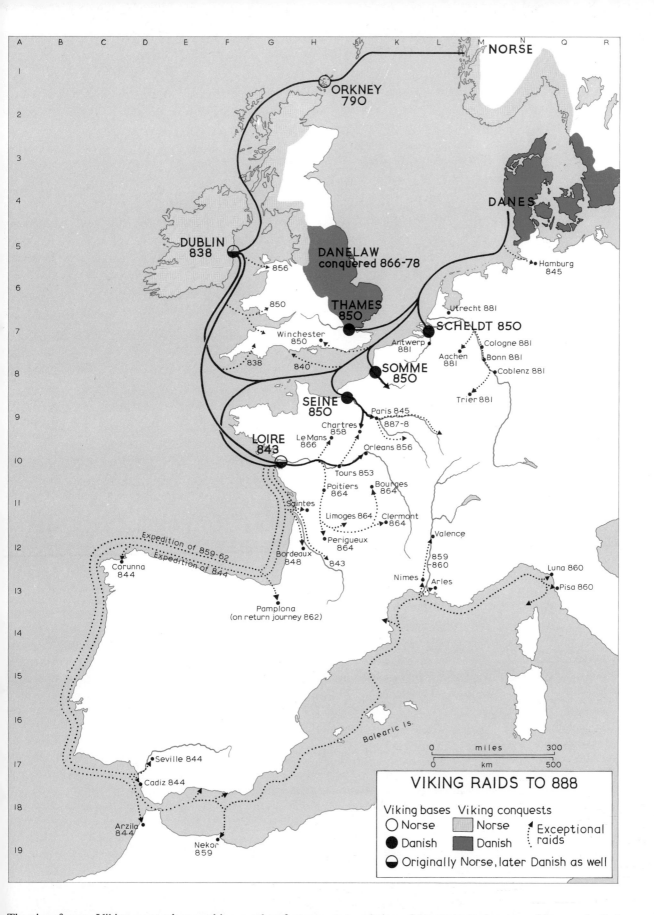

VIKING RAIDS TO 888

Viking bases
○ Norse
● Danish
◐ Originally Norse, later Danish as well

Viking conquests
Norse
Danish

⌁ Exceptional raids

The aim of every Viking was to do something worthy of a saga – a saga being a long poem made up to celebrate a deed of unusual bravery or daring. A good example of the stuff of which sagas were made is shown on the map: Bjorn Ironside's raid into the Mediterranean. This was a running fight spread over three years that took in lands and seas which no Viking had seen before. The highpoint was the sack of a city which Bjorn claimed was Rome. From other sources we know it was only the little town of Luna but one can forgive Bjorn for pitching his claims high: he had to live up to his father, the legendary Ragnar Lothbrok, who figured in so many sagas that he must have been both a great warrior and a really talented liar.

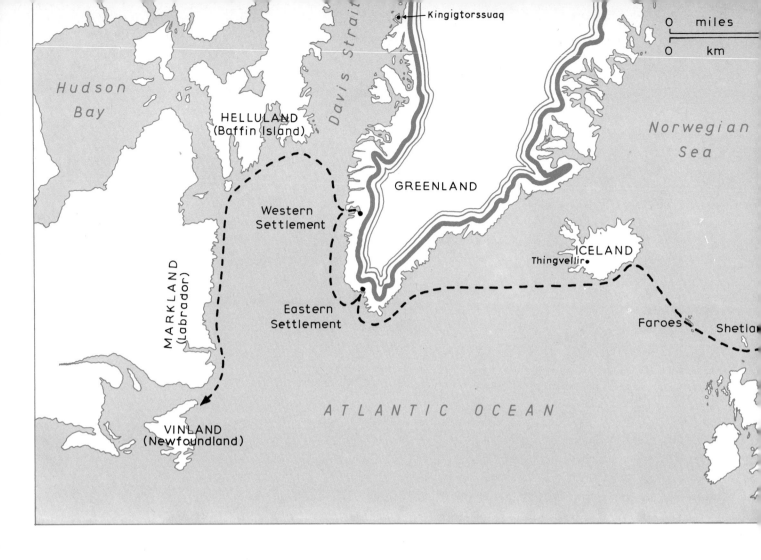

Kingigtorssuaq

miles

km

Hudson Bay

HELLULAND (Baffin Island)

Davis Strait

GREENLAND

Norwegian Sea

Western Settlement

ICELAND
Thingvellir

MARKLAND (Labrador)

Eastern Settlement

Faroes

Shetla

VINLAND (Newfoundland)

ATLANTIC OCEAN

The Norse in the Atlantic 860-1000

The Norse enjoyed plunder but they wanted land to settle still more.

In Ireland they heard about a big island to the north where no one lived except a few Irish hermits. This was Iceland. The Norse looked it over in the 860s, found the climate no worse than Norway's and began to move in right away. By the mid 10th century Iceland had a thriving Norse settlement.

Greenland was first sighted by a Norse captain who got blown past Iceland. No one followed up his story for fifty years. Then Eric the Red, banished from Iceland for three years for murder, decided to spend his exile looking into it. In the course of his exploration (982–5) Eric found a spot where settlement seemed just possible and on his return to Iceland he painted a glowing picture of his discovery. He also thought up the name Greenland, which is not one that would naturally come to mind for a land almost totally covered by ice. Enough Icelanders believed Eric to help him establish his 'Eastern settlement' (actually just to the west of the south cape). Ten years later a

'Western settlement' was founded further up the coast.

North America was discovered as Greenland was – by accident. Eric's son Leif followed up this tale in or around the year 1000. The first stretches of coastline he sailed along were forbidding – he named them Helluland (Land of Stones) and Markland (Land of Forests). But before he turned back he had reached a more promising country – Vinland, the Land of Grapes. This was almost certainly Newfoundland.

A year or two later Eric's second son Thorvald found America had a drawback. It was already inhabited by 'Skraelings' (Esquimaux or Amerindians) who were hostile more often than not. Thorvald was killed by them in Markland and when three boatloads of Icelanders tried to colonize Vinland, the Skraelings made life too hot for them. After three years the Icelanders gave up and sailed home. Although Greenlanders probably continued to make the occasional voyage to Markland for timber, there was no further attempt at colonization.

There were about 30,000 Icelanders, fewer than 3000 Greenlanders. The distances were too great and the resources too few to carry them across the last stage. On the threshold of the New World the saga ended.

44 The tradition of Atlantic exploration outlasted the Viking age. At the end of the 13th century three Greenlanders left this inscription on the island of Kingigtorssuaq in the Davis Strait.

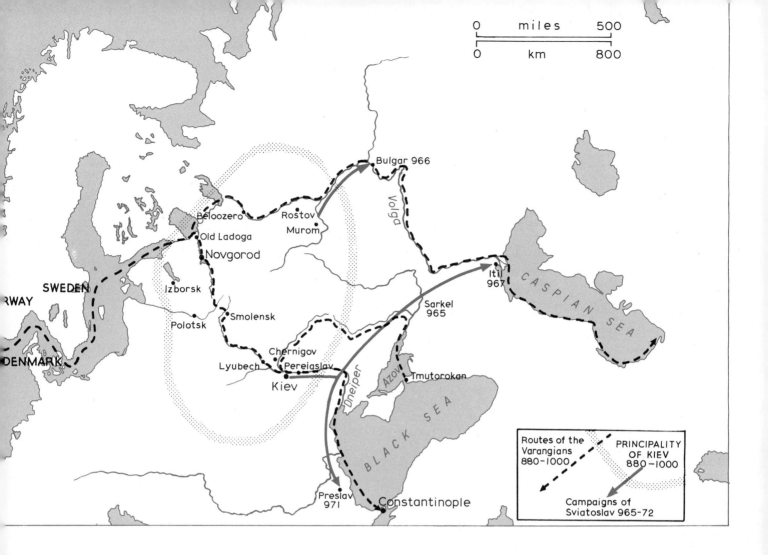

The Swedes in Russia 825-1000

Despite their isolation in the cul-de-sac of the Baltic, the Swedes showed their share of Viking enterprise. In the early 9th century they probed along the great rivers of north Russia and founded the towns of Old Ladoga, Beloozero, Izborsk and Novgorod.[1]

The next generation pushed over the watershed to the rivers that flowed south – great waterways that carried them across the vast extent of European Russia. More towns were founded – Smolensk, Chernigov, Kiev – then the Swedes emerged on the Black Sea (via the Dnieper), on the Sea of Azov (via the Donetz) and on the Caspian (via the Volga).

On and off they tried raiding in the Viking manner. They made a series of attempts on Constantinople, which of course was much too strong for them, and they even attacked the Moslems of the south Caspian. But mostly their efforts went into trade and very successfully, too; they built up a network that not only tapped the resources of Russia but connected north Europe with the ancient trade routes of the Near East.

Their enterprise was also a political success. Soon most of the Slavs of Russia were paying tribute to either Novgorod or Kiev. After 880 all of them were brought into a unified state based on Kiev.

The Vikings in the east were called Varangians or Russians. Nobody is sure what either word means but Russian soon came to mean not a Swede but a Slav: there were so few Swedes that they were bound to become Slav quite quickly. Within a few generations the princes of Kiev were Russian in the modern sense – in fact the third prince was called Sviatoslav, which is hardly a Swedish name.

Sviatoslav was a great fighter. He warred with the Bulgars of the Upper Volga and the Khazars of the Lower Volga and from time to time gave the Byzantines a lot of trouble. He was finally defeated and killed by the Patzinaks – an important event because it stopped the Slavs from trying to colonize the south Russian steppe. They gave up the attempt and withdrew to central Russia. The principality of Kiev settled down with frontiers much less extensive than Sviatoslav had hoped for.

[1] More exactly they turned the Slav villages that already existed on these sites into markets for trade and centres of political control over the tribes around.

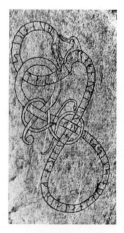

45 Memorial stone put up by Ragnvald in Uppland, Sweden (map 39 D6). On it Ragnvald says that he had served in the Greek (Byzantine) army – presumably in the emperor's crack regiment, the Varangian Guard.

46 Maya warrior

Until immigrants from Europe altered the balance Meso America or 'Middle America' – the area now covered by Mexico, Guatemala and the Honduras – was by far the most important part of the New World. It contained as many people as North and South America together. In our period this would be about three million out of the six million in the New World. There were more Middle Americans because they were full-fledged farmers. The other Amerindians were mostly hunters and fishermen.

Around AD 300 the Middle Americans started to build pyramids. These were like the Sumerian ziggurats rather than the Egyptian pyramids – a flight of steps led up to a temple at the top. Many of the pyramids are so big that they must have been the work of many villages. Whether this united effort was voluntary or enforced by con-

quest we have no way of knowing – the Amerindians had no writing and have left no history.

The pyramid-builders of the south half of Middle America were the Maya. They had a system for inscribing dates so we can tell which of their pyramids were built at this time. In the north the situation is much less clear. There are no dating inscriptions and whether or not a pyramid belongs to this period (which archaeologists call 'Classic') must be decided by excavation. This has only been done for the major pyramid groups like Teotihuacan. We are often unsure which people built the various pyramids, too, for the tribal pattern in the north was later upset by Chichimec immigration (see below).

But the fact that the north of the map has fewer sites marked on it than the south does not mean it was less important. Teotihuacan was twice the

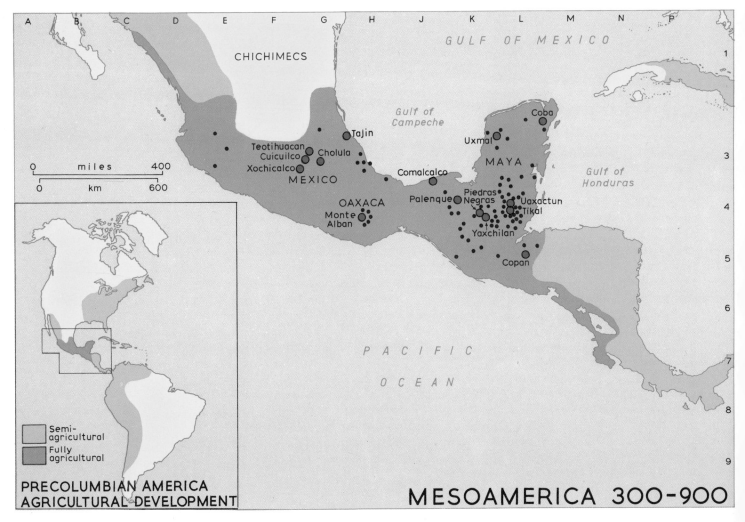

MESOAMERICA 300-900

PRECOLUMBIAN AMERICA
AGRICULTURAL DEVELOPMENT

Semi-agricultural
Fully agricultural

size of any of the Classic Mayan pyramid groups. Its builders were probably already irrigating their fields, which shows that, in agriculture at least, they were far in advance of the Maya.

The Chichimecs were barbarians from the deserts of north Mexico. Around AD 750 they sacked Teotihuacan and settled in the area. All pyramid building ceased. Over the next 100 years it also ceased in the Maya zone, presumably as a result of Chichimec raids. The Classic period – the Amerindians' first attempt at something better than a tribal society – ended in an abrupt return to barbarism.

47 *Top* Maya pyramid at Palenque known as the Temple of the Inscriptions. It is one of the few pyramids with anything inside – it has a crypt containing the sacrophagus of a Mayan chief. Dated AD 692.

48 The ceremonial centre of Teotihuacan looking along 'The Avenue of the Dead' from the piazza in front of the Pyramid of the Moon (the names are modern). To the left of the Avenue is the largest surviving Mesoamerican pyramid, the Pyramid of the Sun. At its base it is as big as the Great Pyramid of Cheops but its slope is gentler and it is only half as high as the Egyptian pyramid.

The temples on the tops of the Mexican pyramids were built of mudbrick and thatch so they have vanished: they probably looked much the same as the Mayan pyramid temples.

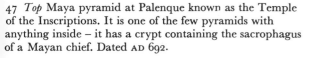

9 BAKTUNS + 7 KATUNS + 17 TUNS + 12 UINALS + 14 KINS

$= 9 \times 144{,}000 + 7 \times 7200 + 17 \times 360 + 12 \times 20 + 14$ DAYS

$= 1{,}296{,}000 + 50{,}400 + 6120 + 240 + 14$ DAYS

$= 1{,}352{,}774$ DAYS

$= 3704$ YEARS SINCE 3113 BC OR 591 AD

49 Mayan relief with a dating inscription on the rim. The Maya used two different calendars: the one on the right-hand side of this relief is a good example of the simpler one. It gives the date in terms of the number of years since 3113 BC (which the Maya believed was the year of creation). The numbers are straightforward – a dot stands for one and a bar for five. The hieroglyphs give the time-periods: a kin is a day, a uinal 20 days, a tun 18 uinals, a katun 20 tuns and a baktun 20 katuns.

The Break-up of the Caliphate 747-1000

50 Coin of al-Muktadir, the 18th Abbasid caliph (908-32)

By the 740s the Umayyads were getting very unpopular in the Arab world.

There was a strong party (known as the Shia, which simply means 'party') who believed that the caliphate rightly belonged to the descendants of Ali, the son-in-law of the Prophet. Other Arab factions had claims of their own or simply resented the Umayyads' monopoly of power.

In 747 a revolt broke out in Khorasan, the northeast province of Persia. By 750 the rebels had placed Abu al Abbas, a descendant of an uncle of the Prophet, on the throne of the caliphs. Abbas 'the bloodthirsty' earned his title by killing every member of the Umayyad clan he could lay hands on. Except for one Umayyad prince who escaped to Spain the massacre was complete.

Under the new Abbasid line the Arab Empire ceased to expand. Indeed the empire actually became smaller because the Abbasids lost control of the provinces in the far west. In Spain the Umayyad prince Abd al Rahman established an independent emirate. In Morocco the Shia seized power and set up a rival caliph.

All the same if the Abbasid Empire was not quite as big as the Umayyad it was still very big indeed. Its armies were strong, its revenues huge and its court luxurious. The fourth Abbasid ruler, Haroun al Raschid, has passed into folklore as the caliph to whom Scheherazade told the stories of the Thousand and One Nights. The fairy-tale image is not inappropriate for the early Abbasids.

Because Syria was pro-Umayyad the Abbasids based themselves on Iraq. There they built a series of capitals (see pp. 58-9), of which Bagdad is the most famous and the one most of them preferred. As a result of this move east the caliphate became more and more Persian in style and outlook. Provinces far from Persia were neglected. In 800, when Haroun al Raschid gave Ibn Aghlab the emirate of 'Africa' (modern Tunisia) he also gave him the right to pass the emirate on to his son. In effect he was allowing Africa to become an independent principality.

Giving away Tunisia did the caliphate little direct harm. Tunisia ran at a financial loss because of the constant border wars with the Idrisids of Morocco. However, the action encouraged other governors to try to make their emirates into principalities too. Until well into the 9th century the caliphs kept a firm grip on provincial affairs, then within a few decades they completely lost control. The emirs stopped sending revenue to the central government. They became independent

Islam's gains and losses in the period 800-1000 were small. In the 9th century Sicily and Sardinia were conquered by the Aghlabids of Africa and Crete by freebooters from Egypt. Cyprus and Armenia were lost. In the 10th century there were marginal losses in northern Spain and on the frontier with Byzantium and the Byzantines regained Crete. In the east the Saffarids conquered the kingdoms of Kabul and Zabul in Afghanistan around 870. This gave Islam possession of the Khyber Pass, a much better gateway into India than the south coast route. On the other hand Transoxiana was lost when the pagan Ghuzz Turks overthrew the Samanids.

Arab seamen dominated the Mediterranean in the years between 850 and 950. During this period they sacked most of the Christian towns within reach of the sea (including Rome, but not Constantinople) and they even established bases ashore in the south of France and Italy. The revival of European and Byzantine sea-power caused a rapid fall-off in this raiding after 950: by the year 1000 the Arabs were definitely on the defensive.

princes like the Aghlabids. When the emirs of Egypt and east Persia broke away the caliphate was left with only Iraq and west Persia.

The independent emirs had local tastes, particularly in Persia. The Samanid emirs of Transoxiana were soon using Persian instead of Arabic in official documents.

The heyday of this Persian revival was the 10th century. By the end of it Persian princes of the Buwayhid clan had taken over Iraq and west Persia and the caliph himself was under their orders. The later Abbasid caliphate was less important than the caliphate founded by the Fatimids in Africa.[1] Indeed the Abbasids had become less important than their old rivals, the Umayyad emirs of Spain – who now began to call themselves caliphs again.

The simple reason for the rapid decline of the Abbasids is that they let the provincial governors become too powerful. The decline of the Arabs as a ruling caste is a more general problem. Partly, as happens to any conquering minority, they were absorbed into the much larger mass of the conquered. Partly the puritan ideals of Islam – the belief that simple things are best – encouraged the Arabs of Arabia to keep to the primitive life of their barren peninsula. This deprived the caliphate of the man-power it needed. When most of Arabia was seized by the Qarmatians, a Shia sect who despised the Abbasids, the Bedouin actually became enemies of the caliph.

But in strictly military terms the Arabs had anyway met their match. When the later Abbasids hired guards it was not Arabs they chose but Turks. Though emirs might be Arab or Persian by the 10th century, the armies were Turkish.

We know from China's history where this leads. In 994 a Turkish general set himself up as emir of Afghanistan. Five years later the Turks of the steppe wiped out the Persians of Transoxiana. The whole northeast frontier of Islam was torn wide open and Turkish tribes began to move their flocks on to the Iranian plateau.

[1] The Fatimids were the leaders of the Shia in Tunisia. They had overthrown the Aghlabid emirs in 909 and then gone on to conquer Egypt and Palestine in 969-72.

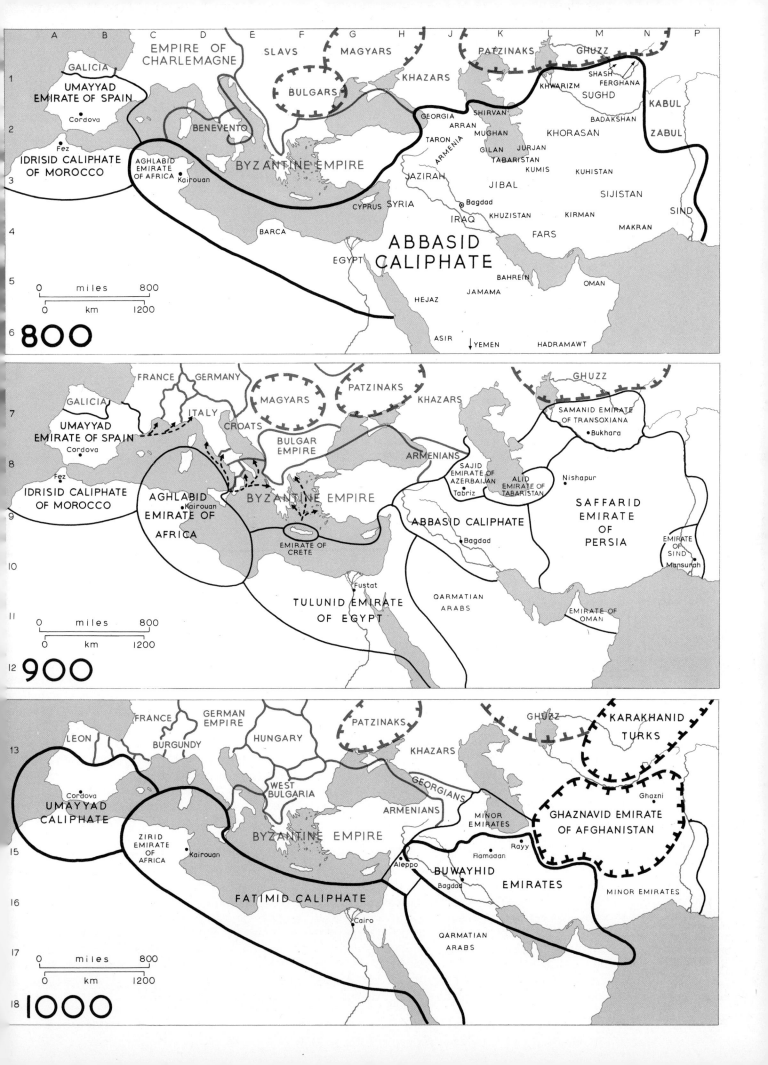

Map 1 — 800

GALICIA
EMPIRE OF CHARLEMAGNE
SLAVS
MAGYARS
PATZINAKS
GHUZZ
UMAYYAD EMIRATE OF SPAIN
Cordova
BULGARS
KHAZARS
SHASH
FERGHANA
KWARIZM
SUGHD
KABUL
Fez
BENEVENTO
GEORGIA
ARRAN
SHIRVAN
BADAKSHAN
ZABUL
IDRISID CALIPHATE OF MOROCCO
AGHLABID EMIRATE OF AFRICA
Kairouan
BYZANTINE EMPIRE
TARON
ARMENIA
MUGHAN
GILAN
JURJAN
KHORASAN
JAZIRAH
TABARISTAN
KUMIS
KUHISTAN
CYPRUS
SYRIA
Bagdad
JIBAL
SIJISTAN
BARCA
IRAQ
KHUZISTAN
KIRMAN
SIND
EGYPT
FARS
MAKRAN
ABBASID CALIPHATE
BAHREIN
OMAN
HEJAZ
JAMAMA
miles 800
km 1200
ASIR
YEMEN
HADRAMAWT

800

Map 2 — 900

FRANCE
GERMANY
GHUZZ
GALICIA
ITALY
MAGYARS
PATZINAKS
KHAZARS
SAMANID EMIRATE OF TRANSOXIANA
UMAYYAD EMIRATE OF SPAIN
Cordova
CROATS
BULGAR EMPIRE
ARMENIANS
Bukhara
Fez
IDRISID CALIPHATE OF MOROCCO
AGHLABID EMIRATE OF AFRICA
Kairouan
BYZANTINE EMPIRE
SAJID EMIRATE OF AZERBAIJAN
Tabriz
ALID EMIRATE OF TABARISTAN
Nishapur
SAFFARID EMIRATE OF PERSIA
EMIRATE OF CRETE
ABBASID CALIPHATE
Bagdad
EMIRATE OF SIND
Mansurah
Fustat
TULUNID EMIRATE OF EGYPT
QARMATIAN ARABS
EMIRATE OF OMAN
miles 800
km 1200

900

Map 3 — 1000

FRANCE
GERMAN EMPIRE
PATZINAKS
GHUZZ
KARAKHANID TURKS
LEON
BURGUNDY
HUNGARY
KHAZARS
Cordova
WEST BULGARIA
GEORGIANS
UMAYYAD CALIPHATE
ARMENIANS
MINOR EMIRATES
GHAZNAVID EMIRATE OF AFGHANISTAN
Ghazni
ZIRID EMIRATE OF AFRICA
Kairouan
BYZANTINE EMPIRE
Aleppo
Rayy
Hamadan
BUWAYHID
Bagdad
EMIRATES
MINOR EMIRATES
FATIMID CALIPHATE
Cairo
QARMATIAN ARABS
miles 800
km 1200

1000

The Byzantine Empire 600-1025

51 Byzantine emperor

Originally the Eastern Roman Empire had five armies at its disposal – the armies of Illyria, Thrace and the East (on the frontiers) and two Guard armies (held in reserve at Constantinople).

Justinian created a new army for the defence of the Armenian frontier (map 13) and at some time the two Guard armies were combined. Otherwise the system remained the same until the near-collapse of the empire in the reign of the emperor Heraclius (map 19).

Heraclius faced a situation in which the Balkans had been overrun by the Avars and Slavs while the eastern provinces were falling one after another to the Persians. The army of Illyria had disintegrated, the army of the East had been pushed back to the Taurus. And to cap it all there was no money in the treasury.

Heraclius saw that the empire had one asset left – Anatolia. Here was a block of twenty provinces that had so far escaped devastation. They must be used to maintain the armies, and the armies must be used to defend them. Except for the capital, Europe was written off. The Thracian command was broken up and its regiments transferred to the army of the East. This left three armies: the Guard in Constantinople and the Armenian and Eastern commands on the Persian front. Each was given half a dozen of the Anatolian provinces as an area of responsibility and as a source of recruits and supplies. Now the struggle could be sustained even though the treasury stayed empty.[1]

The new areas of responsibility were known as 'themes', from the Greek word for an army command. Shortly after the creation of the themes the old provinces were abolished. With them went the civilian administration. The post-Heraclian empire – the Byzantine Empire as historians call it – was ruled by generals.

Heraclius' reform worked: the themes he organized for the Persian war saw the empire through the even more crushing defeats inflicted by the Arabs. By 700 what was left of the empire in Europe had been reorganized in the same way – into the three themes of Thrace, Greece and Sicily.

The system had its drawbacks. A general commanding an army and the resources of half a dozen provinces was a much more powerful man than the old provincial governor. The commander of a theme could defy the emperor himself. And as the Heraclian dynasty drew to its end the theme commanders began to fight each other for the

[1] The troops still had to be paid if they served outside their area of responsibility. Heraclius was able to launch his counter-offensive only because the Church advanced him the money.

throne. As you might expect the winner was the general of the biggest theme, the Anatolikon as the army of the East was now called.

It was in 717 that Leo, commander of the Anatolikon, became the emperor Leo III. He beat off the second Arab attack on Constantinople and founded a new line of emperors that lasted for the remainder of the century. They protected themselves from revolts by dividing up the themes.

Leo started with his old theme, the Anatolikon, where he re-established the independence of the Thracian units (the new theme was called the Thracesion to distinguish it from Thrace proper). Next the theme of the Guard was divided between the three Guard regiments – Opsikion, Brucellarion and Optimation. By 950 the four themes in Anatolia had become fourteen and were getting too small to support army units that could be dangerous to either friend or enemy.

The pressure on the Byzantine Empire slackened off during the 10th century so the division of the themes didn't bring disaster. In fact the sort of defence-in-depth the themes provided was no longer needed. The empire's enemies had weakened and the time had come for a counter-offensive. The Byzantines began to build up a striking force capable of exploiting the favourable situation.

This new army was given first call on the resources of the themes. As it contained a good many foreign mercenaries who had to be paid in cash the emperor was soon asking the themes for money not men. The theme regiments dwindled as the striking force expanded. After a 300-year gap the empire was returning to the old Roman system of tax-paying provinces (for that is what the themes now became) and a paid army.

The first important victory for the new army was the conquest of Melitene in the 930s. Then came the recovery of Crete (960), Cilicia (965), Antioch (969) and east Bulgaria (971). In 1018 the emperor Basil II conquered west Bulgaria. Once again the Danube became the empire's frontier in Europe. In the east, Aleppo and Damascus were made to pay tribute and imperial forces were able to mop up most of the dozen Armenian principalities.

At this point the empire looked stronger than it had for centuries. The new army had been a great success. It had to be, for now the theme units had been allowed to run down the empire depended on it absolutely.

48

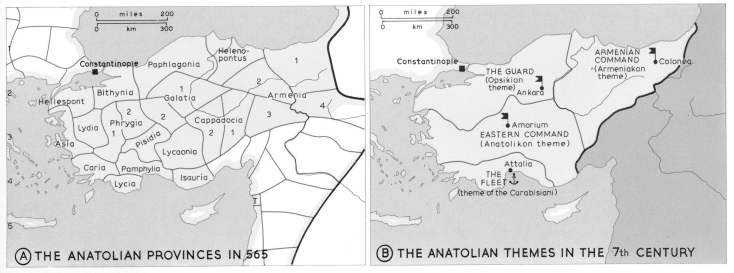

(A) THE ANATOLIAN PROVINCES IN 565

(B) THE ANATOLIAN THEMES IN THE 7th CENTURY

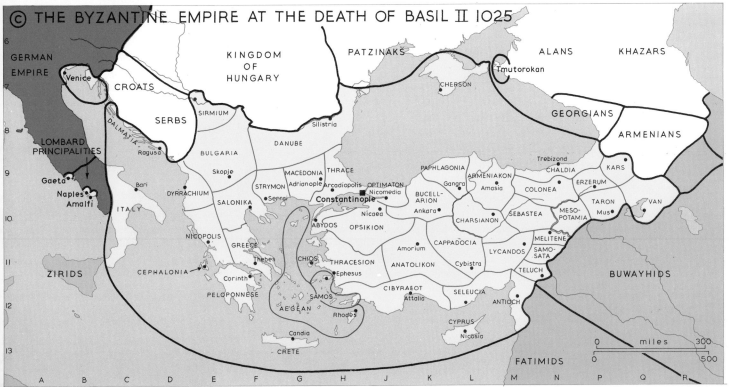

(C) THE BYZANTINE EMPIRE AT THE DEATH OF BASIL II 1025

52

53

THE ARMENIANS

For most of its history Armenia has been the battleground of rival empires. At first it was the Romans versus the Persians, then Byzantines versus Arabs. But in the late 9th century the Arabs withdrew and the Byzantines only gradually moved forward to take their place. Armenia enjoyed a brief spell of independence.

The Armenians were zealous Christians and they celebrated this good fortune with a burst of church building. Armenian architects worked out new variations of the centrally-planned church. They acquired such prestige that when the dome of S. Sophia fell in 989 the Byzantines sent for an Armenian architect to repair it.

Armenia soon became a battleground again so few of the churches of this period remain. The one illustrated (52), the Church of the Holy Cross on the islet of Aght'amar in Lake Van, only survives because of its out-of-the-way location. It was built in 915–21 as part of his palace by King Gagik who ruled the Lake Van region at this time. The drawing (53), copied from a relief on the outside of the church, shows Gagik holding a model of the building. This is a standard way of representing a church's donor.

China reunited
900-1000

The general who put an end to the T'ang dynasty was Chu Wen. Originally a small-time bandit, he joined the peasant rebel leader Huang Ch'ao and rose to be one of his commanders. Then he went over to the government.

His reward was the governorship of K'aifeng which made him one of the thirty or so war lords who were the real rulers of China. Gradually Chu Wen increased the area under his control. By 907 he held both imperial capitals and was able to make himself emperor.

Chu Wen's dynasty did not last long. He had built up his power by skilful politics and his forces were not really a match for the Turko-Mongol armies of the north frontier. In 923 the northern armies, led by the Turks of the T'ai-yuan command, deposed Chu Wen's successor and placed their own candidate on the throne.

The armies, determined to keep their emperor under control, stayed in the capital. There they formed a 'palace army' which – bar the army of the Kitan Mongols – had no rival in China. But this army was never used. Quarrels among the Turkish chieftains and the intervention of the Kitans prevented any of the short-lived Turkish emperors from exercising its power. Then in 960

Chao K'uang-yin, commander of the palace army, seized the throne. By 979 he and his successor had conquered the six kingdoms of the south and founded the Sung dynasty. The Sung emperors were to rule most of China for the next 300 years.[1]

The Sung Empire was not really as strong as it looks on the map. The Kitan Mongols had seized the northeast in 937 and the Sung were badly defeated when they tried to get it back. Peace was bought only at the price of an annual tribute. Kitan power spread over the whole of Inner Mongolia. In 1009 the Kitan emperors (who called themselves the Liao dynasty) conquered Kansu. Though the Sung ruled nearly all China they never held the frontier areas usually considered necessary for China's security.

But if the Sung never earned any military glory, by paying tribute to the northern nomads they bought the dynasty as long a life as any other dynasty got by fighting. They also bought peace and good Confucian government again for the mass of Chinese people. The Sung period was to be one of great and increasing prosperity.

---

[1] Chao K'uang-yin came from a Hopei military family and was presumably of Turko-Mongol descent. But the dynasty he founded is considered purely Chinese for the same reasons as is the T'ang (see p. 30).

The Chinese call the fifty years between the T'ang and Sung the 'Five Dynasties period'. Chu Wen's Liang dynasty is one, the next three – known as the Later T'ang, Chin and Han – were founded by other Turkish generals. The last, the Chou, was like its Sung successor founded by a commander of the palace army.

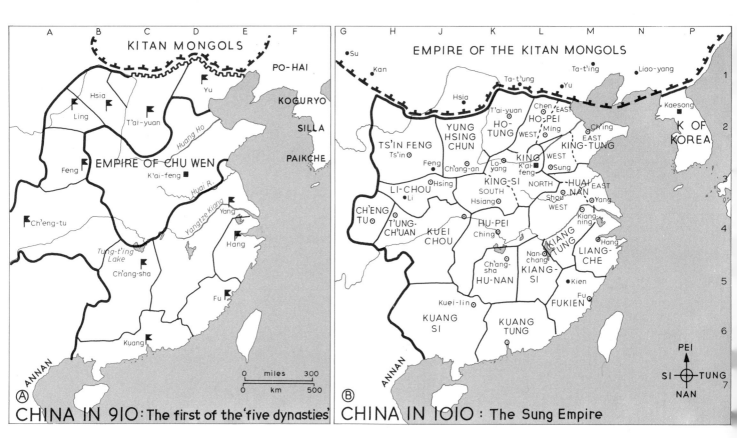

CHINA IN 910: The first of the 'five dynasties'

CHINA IN 1010: The Sung Empire

Set prayers are a part of every religion. And most religions agree that if a prayer is worth saying once it must be better to say it twice. The Buddhists carried the idea of repetition to its logical conclusion and were quite happy to use mechanical means of repeating prayers.

The most famous example is the prayer-wheel, which Buddhists believe 'says' the prayer inscribed on its rim every time it is turned. In China the Buddhists quickly developed the idea of printing from the inked stamps that bureaucrats used in their paper work. By the 8th century the Far East was flooded with Buddhist charms printed from wood or copper blocks. Some of these charms were simple line drawings of the Buddha (54), others were short texts (55). Printing had arrived – and in a big way.

To reproduce a Buddhist image or text was considered equivalent to contemplating the Buddha or saying the prayer. So whereas the present-day publisher thinks of how many copies he can sell and prints accordingly, sheer exhaustion was the only factor limiting a Buddhist edition. No less than a million copies of the charm in photo 55 were printed. Only royal funds could afford an act of piety on such a scale: this particular printing was carried out on the orders of the Japanese empress Shotoku (in 770). But Buddhists always thought in big numbers, bigger than any western printer was to achieve until modern times.[1]

A single block can carry only a brief text; printing anything longer than a paragraph means using two or more blocks. There is nothing complicated about this and the Chinese probably started producing multi-block 'books' as soon as they started printing at all. Until recently the oldest example known was a 7-block scroll found at Tun-huang, Kansu (56). It is a copy of a Buddhist text called the Diamond Sutra and bears a date equivalent to AD 868. In 1966 another version of the Diamond Sutra was found in a Korean stupa known to have been completed in 751 (57). This 12-block scroll is currently the oldest known printed 'book'. Indeed it is the oldest known block-print of any sort.

The Chinese bureaucrats frowned on Buddhism which they saw as a threat to their Confucian ideals. So at first they were against printing too. They even passed laws against it. But soon they realized that printing would solve one of their perennial problems: how to get accurate copies of the classics for the administration's training colleges. Manuscript copies inevitably contained a lot of mistakes but if the wood blocks were first checked by good scholars, the printed books would be almost error-free. By Sung times other books besides the classics were being printed. The pages were now bound up in a proper book shape either with a one-side binding like ours today or concertina-style, a method the Chinese preferred (58).

The Chinese book market was always small because most Chinese could not read and the books were too expensive for most of those who could. The Buddhist charms on the other hand were treasured by the common people and the fact that they could not read them did not matter: they were not meant to be read. Printing may now be a means of passing on information but its origins are in a world of magic and superstition.

[1] There was no printing at all in the west before the 15th century.

54

55

56

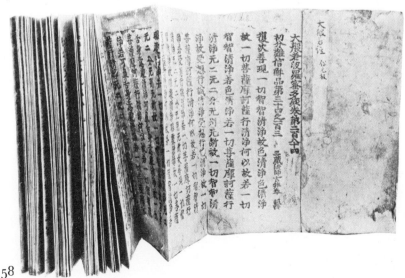

58

Christendom recovers
860-1000

59 Otto III, German emperor, 983–1002

After 500 years of retreat Christendom got back its confidence in the 9th century.

The Orthodox Church of the Byzantine Empire was the first to take the offensive. Two highly successful missions converted the Bulgars and Serbs of the Balkans, a third started work among the Slavs of Bohemia away to the north. The Catholics of the west soon took over here and in the end the Bohemians (and the Croats) joined the Western rather than the Eastern Church. The missionaries from Rome and Constantinople might have done even better if they had co-operated more and quarrelled less. Nevertheless, it was heartening that by 900 both churches were on the move again. At last Christendom had some gains in Europe to set off against its huge losses in the Mediterranean.

The Christian advance received a setback when the Magyars moved into Europe. Driven from the Russian steppe by the Patzinak Turks the Magyars, like the Huns and Avars before them, settled on the plains of Hungary (896). In 899 they mounted their first big raid – against Italy. The army of the kingdom of Italy was totally defeated by the nomads' tactics. For the next fifty years the Magyars were able to plunder the peninsula whenever they felt like it.

The rest of continental Europe suffered almost as severely. Germany was raided almost every year and some Magyar bands even reached France and Spain. Not until 955 when the German king Otto I trapped and destroyed the main Magyar army at Lechfeld was Europe freed from their devastations.

The prestige Otto I gained by this victory helped him in his main work – the re-creation of Charlemagne's empire. In 961 he conquered the kingdom of Italy. The next year the Pope revived the title of emperor for him. France and Burgundy remained outside the empire, but on the other hand Otto conquered the Slavs on the empire's east border. Otto's empire suffered from the same defects as Charlemagne's – it had almost no administrative structure. But its outline was to become the central feature in the map of medieval Europe.

This map was now taking shape. The kings of Wessex conquered the Danish settlers and created the kingdom of England. The kingdom of Scotland was formed by the union of Scots and Picts (844) and Strathclyde Welsh (945). Both these kingdoms owed their unity to the pressure of Viking attacks.

The Vikings themselves were getting more organized: the three kingdoms of Scandinavia were permanent by the early 10th century and were officially, if half-heartedly, Christian by the year 1000.

The same year saw the final victory of the Catholic Church in central Europe. There the Poles and Magyars had been hanging back because they did not want to be under German archbishops. The emperor Otto III agreed that their objection was reasonable and saw to it that they got archbishoprics of their own. He also recognized the duke of the Magyars as king of Hungary (Hungary means 'Land of the Huns': the Magyars were not unreasonably thought to be linear descendants of Attila's Huns).[1]

In Kiev, on the far edge of Europe, Sviatoslav's son Prince Vladimir hesitated between Eastern and Western Churches. In 980 he sent ambassadors to Constantinople via Germany. They returned to report that in the German churches 'there was no glory' but that in Constantinople, in Santa Sophia 'we knew not whether we were in heaven or on earth . . . we cannot forget that beauty'. Vladimir demanded and obtained a Byzantine bride and was received into the Orthodox faith. The old idols of Kiev were cast into the Dnieper and the Prince's obedient subjects herded after them in compulsory baptism.

Few centuries in European history have started as dismally as the 10th. North Europe was being ravaged by pagan Vikings, south Europe by Moslem sea raiders, the centre by the Magyars. Few have ended so triumphantly, as the frontier of Christendom surged eastward from the Elbe to the Volga. Many Christians had believed that the year 1000 would see the end of the world. In fact it saw the end of the Dark Ages.

---

[1] The Eastern Church kept tight control of its satellites. The Bulgars in their heyday had been able to insist on their Church being independent but this patriarchate of Ochrid was suppressed by the Byzantines when they conquered east Bulgaria (1018). The bishops of Kiev were always Greeks, sent out by the patriarch of Constantinople.

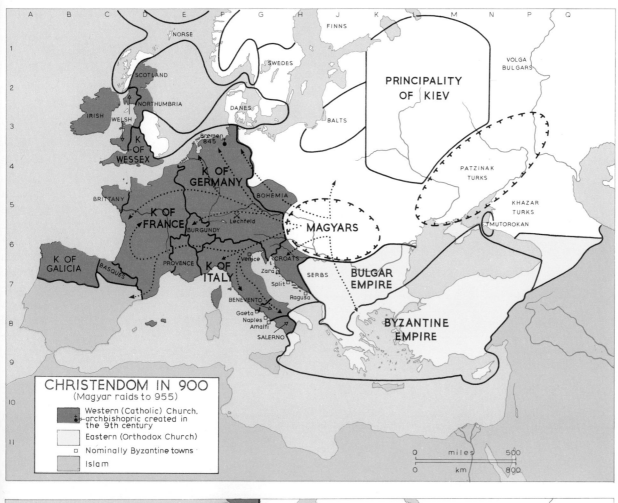

A B C D E F G H J K L M N P Q

NORSE

FINNS

SWEDES

PRINCIPALITY
OF KIEV

VOLGA
BULGARS

SCOTLAND

NORTHUMBRIA

DANES

BALTS

IRISH

WELSH

K
OF
WESSEX

Bremen
845

K OF
GERMANY

BOHEMIA

PATZINAK
TURKS

BRITTANY

K OF
FRANCE

Lechfeld

MAGYARS

KHAZAR
TURKS

BURGUNDY

TMUTOROKAN

K OF
GALICIA

BASQUES

PROVENCE

K OF
ITALY

Venice

CROATS

Zara

SERBS

BULGAR
EMPIRE

BENEVENTO

Split

Ragusa

Gaeta
Naples
Amalfi

BYZANTINE
EMPIRE

SALERNO

CHRISTENDOM IN 900
(Magyar raids to 955)

■ Western (Catholic) Church,
archbishopric created in
the 9th century

☐ Eastern (Orthodox Church)

☐ Nominally Byzantine towns

Islam

0 — miles — 500
0 — km — 800

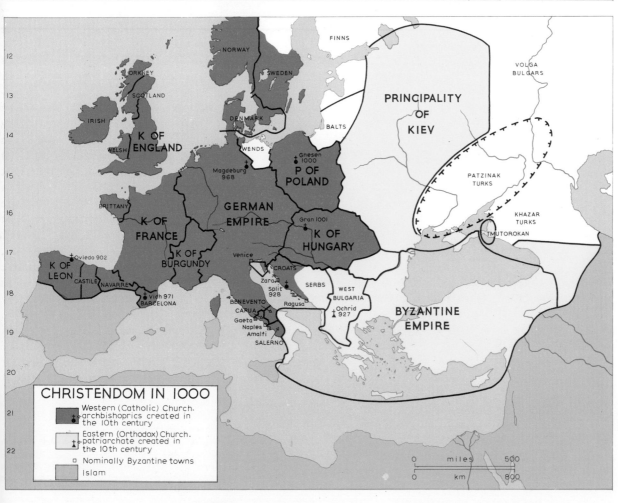

NORWAY

FINNS

VOLGA
BULGARS

ORKNEY

SWEDEN

SCOTLAND

IRISH

K OF
ENGLAND

DENMARK

BALTS

PRINCIPALITY
OF
KIEV

WELSH

WENDS

Gnesen
1000

P OF
POLAND

Magdeburg
968

GERMAN
EMPIRE

PATZINAK
TURKS

BRITTANY

K OF
FRANCE

Gran 1001

K OF
HUNGARY

KHAZAR
TURKS

K OF
BURGUNDY

Venice

CROATS

TMUTOROKAN

K OF
LEON

Oviedo 902

CASTILE

NAVARRE

Zara
Split
928

SERBS

WEST
BULGARIA

Vich 971
BARCELONA

BENEVENTO

CAPUA

Ragusa

Ochrid
927

BYZANTINE
EMPIRE

Gaeta
Naples
Amalfi

SALERNO

CHRISTENDOM IN 1000

■ Western (Catholic) Church,
archbishoprics created in
the 10th century

☐ Eastern (Orthodox) Church,
patriarchate created in
the 10th century

☐ Nominally Byzantine towns

Islam

0 — miles — 500
0 — km — 800

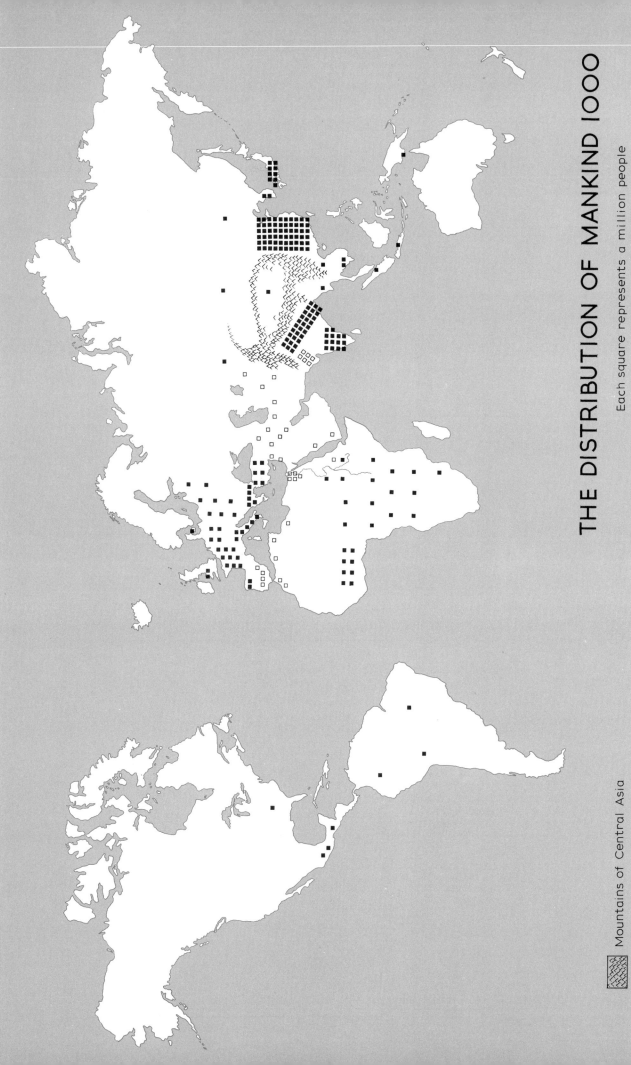

THE DISTRIBUTION OF MANKIND 1000

Each square represents a million people

□ Mohammedan   ■ Others

▨ Mountains of Central Asia

The End of the Dark Ages

The Dark Ages is a term invented to cover west European history between 400 and 1000. During this period Europe almost ceased to produce the sort of evidence historians need. Hardly anyone kept an account of what was going on – for many times and places we have no records at all. The age is dark in the sense that we know much less about it than we do about the periods before and after.

Historians who study west European art of this time also have very little to go on. There is practically nothing in our museums except weapons and jewellery. As for architecture, there isn't any to speak of. The Dark Ages are not only dark for us, looking back: they were dark for the people at the time. Society was less literate and less well ordered than it had been in Roman times. And the fact that it left so little behind shows how poorly people lived.

To what extent can the Dark Ages be considered a world-wide phenomenon? Obviously the term does not apply to the Arabs: this was their great age. Nor to the Chinese: during the T'ang period they developed their classical culture to its all-time high. It will do for Byzantium which went through a very bad patch in the 7th to 9th centuries. And it fits India exactly. There the collapse of the Gupta Empire in the 5th century was followed by 500 years of which almost nothing is known (see below). But if we mean cultural decline it would be wrong to say this was a Dark Age for mankind generally. Taking the world as a whole the situation was maintained or even a little improved.

This sounds not too bad but it is in fact an argument for using a term like 'Dark Ages' in world history. For in the periods before and after this mankind did much better. The common feature of the centuries between 400 and 1000 is that the rate of advance was drastically slowed. This is clearly shown in the figures for world population.

The total increase over the period 400–1000 was from 205 million to 235 million – or 15%. In the previous 600 years the increase had been near enough 100 per cent and it was to be 100 per cent again in the following 600 years.[1] Nowadays we are worried about too many people and too rapid a rate of population growth (rightly so – a 100 per cent increase takes less than 60 years now, not 600). But at a time when the world had too few people and its resources were too little used, a static population meant that society was not getting on top of its problems – human, economic and technical.

[1] The figures are, of course, only estimates but we don't think they have been influenced by our thesis. Most historians believe that European and Mediterranean populations were actually *below* their Roman levels during the Dark Ages. As for China we have census figures from Han, T'ang and early Sung times which indicate the population was essentially static. Between them these areas account for half the population of the world at the time.

INDIA IN THE DARK AGES

Although we know very little about India in the Dark Ages we do know that this period saw an important change. Buddhism declined and Hinduism, the old Indian way of looking at the world, once again came to dominate the sub-continent. Buddhism retained its hold only at the edges of the country.

If you think of India as a diamond the areas that clung to Buddhism longest are at the points: Sind, Bengal and Ceylon plus, in the north, the states of the Himalayan fringe. Even here Buddhism showed little vitality. The fiery Moslems easily conquered and converted Sind in the 8th century and in the later medieval period when all north India was in their power the Buddhists of Bengal proved much easier to turn into Moslems than the Hindus of the Indian heartland. Islam's success in these two Buddhist areas and its lack of success in the Hindu centre explain why Pakistan started off as a two-part state.

The reversion to Hinduism and the political break-up of the country are the two most striking features of India in the Dark Ages. With them went a decline in India's standing in the world. In the classical period the Maurya and Gupta empires ranked with Rome and China: now Indian culture became provincial and stagnant.

The little Hindu temple which is one of the period's few monuments illustrates the point. It contains an ante-

60 Parasuramesvara temple, Bhuvanesvar, Orissa

chamber (on the left) and a shrine in a symbolic shape that represents the Hindu view of the world as a mountain. Both chambers are roofed in the simplest way with slabs of stone. This is architecture at the Amerindian level: for a people who had once known the arch it represents a sad decline.

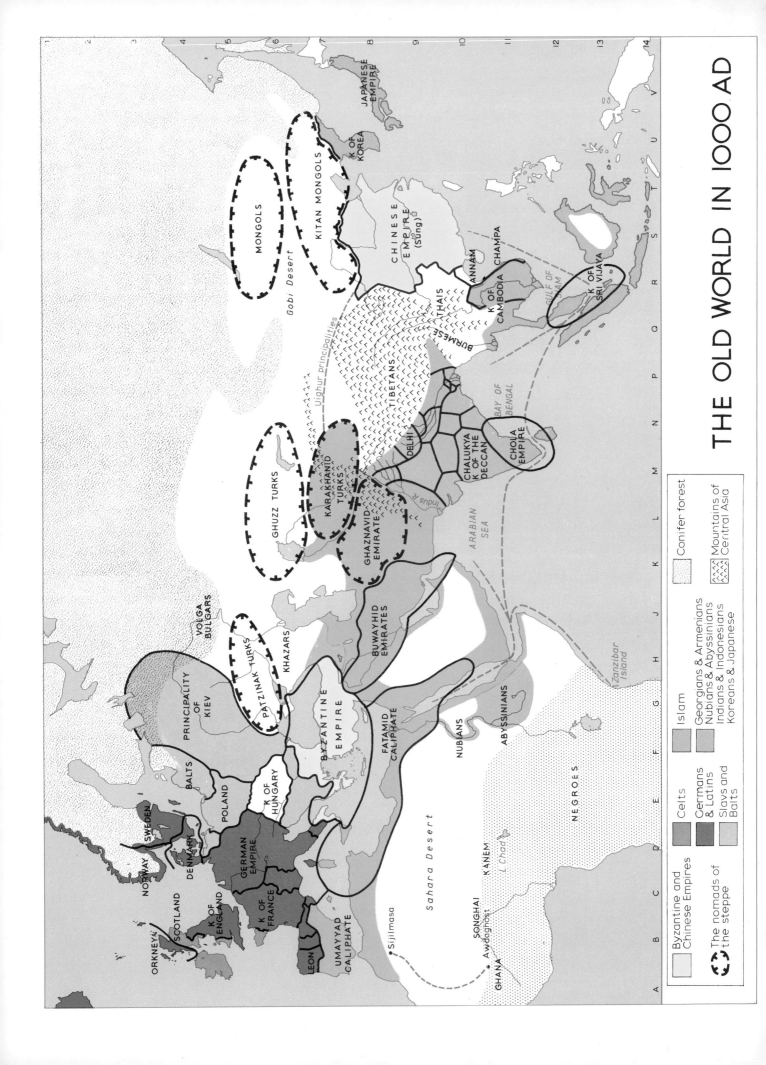

THE OLD WORLD IN 1000 AD

Byzantine and Chinese Empires
The nomads of the steppe
Celts
Germans & Latins
Slavs and Balts
Islam
Georgians & Armenians
Nubians & Abyssinians
Indians & Indonesians
Koreans & Japanese
Conifer forest
Mountains of Central Asia

MONGOLS

KITAN MONGOLS

Gobi Desert

JAPANESE EMPIRE

K OF KOREA

CHINESE EMPIRE (Sung)

ANNAM

Uighur principalities

TIBETANS

BURMESE

THAIS

K OF CAMBODIA

CHAMPA

GULF OF SIAM

K OF SRI VIJAYA

GHUZZ TURKS

KARAKHANID TURKS

GHAZNAVID EMIRATE

DELHI

Indus R.

CHALUKYA K OF THE DECCAN

CHOLA EMPIRE

BAY OF BENGAL

BUWAYHID EMIRATES

ARABIAN SEA

Zanzibar Island

VOLGA BULGARS

PATZINAK TURKS

KHAZARS

PRINCIPALITY OF KIEV

BALTS

BYZANTINE EMPIRE

FATAMID CALIPHATE

NUBANS

ABYSSINIANS

NORWAY

SWEDEN

DENMARK

POLAND

K OF HUNGARY

GERMAN EMPIRE

K OF FRANCE

K OF ENGLAND

SCOTLAND

ORKNEYS

LEON

UMAYYAD CALIPHATE

Sahara Desert

NEGROES

KANEM

L. Chad

SONGHAI

Awdaghost

GHANA

• Sijilmasa

The Old World in 1000

Compare this map of the Old World with the one at the beginning of the book and you will see that only two states have survived the intervening 600 years.

The first prize must go to the Byzantine Empire. At times it had been reduced to little more than the city of Constantinople. But Constantinople had never fallen and the empire had always recovered. It was a great achievement.

The Chinese Empire comes a poor second. All its various capitals had been sacked many times: its emperors had often lost their thrones to barbarian invaders. But the empire had kept on coming together again. In the long run this resilience proved to be the best quality of all.

By contrast India seems to have forgotten its imperial past. The many kings of the subcontinent fought endless indecisive wars. The situation was always in upheaval, yet it never really changed. No one noticed the build-up of the Moslems in the Hindu Kush – the warning sign of an avalanche that would descend on north India in the next century.

This brings us to the new societies – those which did not matter or did not even exist in 400 but had now taken root inside the old empires. First and much the most impressive was Islam, combining Berber, Arab and Persian nations in one faith if no longer under one caliph. Islam had kept up the standards of literacy and urban culture inherited from the Persian and Roman empires and was a worthy successor to the empires of the classical period.

This is more than could be said for western Christendom, the other new society. Almost illiterate and without a significant city, it hardly seems to qualify as a civilization. In fact if its affairs had not picked up in the 10th century one would have to exclude it. Its kings were as quarrelsome as the rajahs of India. The attempts to revive the Roman Empire by Charlemagne and Otto I were just pipe dreams. The only influence towards unity was the Catholic Church, which at least kept Latin alive as a means of communication between peoples.[1]

If the civilized world had done poorly during the Dark Ages, the nomads had done rather well. In Europe they had colonized the Hungarian steppe. In east Persia they had become the dominant force. At the other end of their territory they had conquered China several times over and were currently holding the Sung Empire to ransom.

To some extent these were hollow successes. Conquering nomads usually disappeared in a few generations because they were so few and the peasants they conquered so many. To survive as a people in the agricultural zone they had to become farmers themselves. Hungary, for example, was to become just another of the settled states of Christendom in the 11th century. But in clearing the Slavs off the Russian steppe the Patzinaks won a real if defensive victory – they kept this area of pastureland open for the nomad way of life. The Kitan conquest of Inner Mongolia served the same cause.

Trade routes at the end of the Dark Ages do show some advance on the classical period. There was probably little more traffic – any increase on the Silk Route is likely to have been balanced by a decline on the Spice Route – but almost everywhere the horizon had expanded a little. Scandinavia, Poland and central Russia had been barely known to the Romans – now these regions were definitely part of Christendom. Japan had joined the nations of the Far East. Indonesians as well as Indo-Chinese visited China.

In Africa Moslem traders were in contact with the Negroes south of the Sahara. Regular caravans now set off from Sijilmasa in Morocco carrying copper and general merchandise. In the Sahara they picked up salt from natural deposits. At Awdaghost (in modern Mali) they traded these items for the gold the kings of Ghana got from the tribesmen to the south.[2] We also hear of a Songhai kingdom in the Middle Niger and a kingdom of Kanem round Lake Chad.

These were not the only explorations into the mystery of Africa: on the east coast Arab seamen had sailed as far as Zanzibar and were beginning to set up trading stations.

[1] Although the Germans had conquered west Europe and become its rulers most people in the old Roman areas continued to speak languages derived from Latin. The most important of these 'Romance' languages are French, Spanish and Italian. So though the map shows west Europe as though it was German, remember that only the English, the Scandinavians and the Germans were actually German-speaking.

[2] The modern state of Ghana is on the Gulf of Guinea 800 km to the southeast of medieval Ghana. As the first West African state to gain independence (in 1957) modern Ghana was able to take the name of black Africa's oldest known kingdom. But there is really no connection between the two.

The Cities of Islam 1000

Cities almost vanished from the map of Europe in the Dark Ages. Rome, the biggest city in western Christendom, had a mere 15,000 inhabitants.

By contrast Islam had two cities, Cairo and Bagdad, which were ten times this size. And it had more than a dozen with populations around 30,000.[1] It is this difference which supports Islam's claim to being more civilized than Europe during the Dark Ages.

The Arab caliphate was not a maritime empire: its merchants mistrusted boats and usually traded by caravan. They even sent goods from Cairo to Kairouan by caravan, which must have been less economic than the sea route. An important result of this – and of the general collapse of Mediterranean trading which took place at this time – was that the great seaports of classical times disappeared. New Arab cities took their place but they were all inland. Carthage was replaced by Kairouan, Alexandria by Cairo and Antioch dwindled while Aleppo grew.

Trade and industry are the life-blood of towns today. The Arab towns, especially those on the Silk Route, had a share of both. But most of them were basically centres of government, living off the peasant farmers of the countryside around. The

townsmen did indeed provide certain skilled services to the peasants but these services were not essential. If, as in western Europe, the town authorities got too demanding the peasants could do without them.

So the towns were largely imposed on the countryside by the rulers of the state. They could be sited for purely strategic reasons instead of growing up naturally. Indeed they could rise and decline in a few years purely on a caliph's whim.

This is clearly shown in the Abbasid period. The Abbasids owed their throne to the support of the eastern provinces. Therefore they wanted to move the capital of the empire from Syria to Iraq. But they didn't much mind where in Iraq and they tried several different sites at different times. Bagdad is the one that took root but even after they had founded it (763) the Abbasids did not feel bound to live there. In 836 Caliph al-Mutasim moved upstream and built the entirely new city of Samarra. Fifty-six years later Caliph al-Mutadid moved back to Bagdad. Samarra quickly fell into ruin.

[1] To the twelve on the map one should add Fez and Cordoba in the west.

SAMARRA

The ruins of the city of Samarra extend for some 35 km along the left bank of the Tigris. The northern half built by the tenth Abbasid caliph, al-Mutawakkil, was really a separate city known as al-Jafariya. It was built during the last two years of his reign (860–1) and abandoned on his death. But the remains of Samarra proper are impressive enough without al-Jafariya. The Great Mosque of Samarra is the largest mosque ever built, measuring 240 by 156 m. And yet it is only just visible on the vertical air photo.

61 *Opposite, left* Air view of central Samarra. The dark patch near the Tigris is the modern town which has a population of 16,000. The Great Mosque is at two o'clock from this. The right-hand half of the picture takes in part of the huge Hair attached to the palace of al-Mutamid. The clover leaf is a race-track, the parallel lines are canals marking out the park's main boulevards. Al-Mutasim's palace is at the top of the picture opposite the point where two boulevards converge on the main entrance to the Hair.

62 *Opposite, right* The Great Mosque of which only the outer wall and the minaret remain. The minaret has a spiral rampart that reaches the top in five turns: the architect borrowed the idea from the ziggurat of Babylon which was still in fair condition in his day.

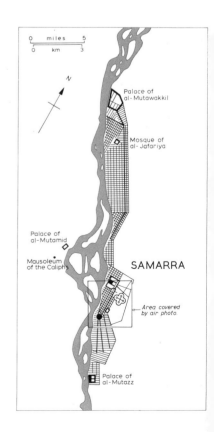

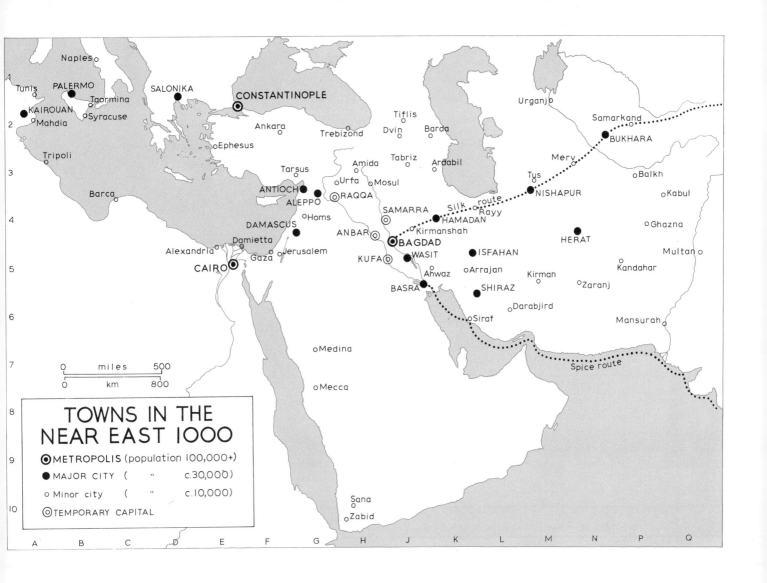

TOWNS IN THE
NEAR EAST 1000

⊙ METROPOLIS (population 100,000+)
● MAJOR CITY (" c.30,000)
○ Minor city (" c.10,000)
◎ TEMPORARY CAPITAL

miles 500
km 800

Naples
Tunis
PALERMO
Taormina
KAIROUAN
Syracuse
Mahdia
Tripoli
SALONIKA
CONSTANTINOPLE
Ankara
Ephesus
Barca
Tarsus
Tiflis
Dvin
Barda
Trebizond
Amida
Tabriz
Ardabil
ANTIOCH
Urfa
Mosul
ALEPPO
RAQQA
Homs
SAMARRA
Rayy
DAMASCUS
ANBAR
Kirmanshah
HAMADAN
Damietta
BAGDAD
Alexandria
Gaza
Jerusalem
KUFA
WASIT
ISFAHAN
CAIRO
Ahwaz
Arrajan
BASRA
SHIRAZ
Darabjird
Siraf
Medina
Mecca
Urganj
Samarkand
BUKHARA
Mery
Balkh
Tus
NISHAPUR
Kabul
Silk route
Ghazna
HERAT
Multan
Kirman
Kandahar
Zaranj
Mansurah
Spice route
Sana
Zabid

A New Beginning

63 The heavy plough which was developed in west Europe. The strange-looking animals pulling it are meant to be oxen

We have seen that when it comes to the civilized life Dark Age Europe was not in the same class as Islam or China.

Yet we know that in the centuries after 1000 western Europe showed a steady economic and cultural growth that eventually put it far ahead of its rivals. So at a time when Europe looked pretty hopeless it was actually changing in a way that was to give it an edge over the rest of the world. What were the changes that gave Europe this advantage?

During the Dark Ages Christendom lost its south Mediterranean lands to Islam and gained territory on its European frontier. The result, as you can see from the map, was a shift north. Christendom had started off as a Mediterranean civilization: in the Dark Ages it became purely European.

The move north was a move to colder, wetter lands. Now agriculture had been invented in the hot dry lands of the Near East and the techniques had all been evolved to get the best yields in that

sort of climate. European farmers took centuries to develop the skills needed to solve their quite different problems. The really important thing that happened in the Dark Ages was that they succeeded. It looked as though Christendom had been pushed into a poor corner of the world: properly exploited it proved to be one of the richest.

The crucial invention was a plough heavy enough to turn and drain the soil, not just scratch a furrow for seed. We know that heavy ploughs were coming into use in north Europe in late Roman times. It took the whole of the Dark Ages to get the design right and in general use. By the year 1000 the European farmer was on top of his job. He couldn't produce as much per hectare as a Near Eastern farmer with irrigated fields but, thanks to his plough, he could produce more in an hour's work. He began to prosper.

This prosperity shows in several ways. Water mills save the farmer the time he would have to spend grinding his wheat. But mills need millers to run them and millers have to be paid. Only a prosperous farming community can afford to do this. It says a great deal about the rising level of prosperity that by the end of the Dark Ages every village in northwest Europe had its water-mill.

Another sign of prosperity is the appearance of the horse as a farm animal. Traditionally ploughing was done with oxen. Horses are more expensive because they eat more but they can work harder and faster. If you can afford them, horses are more profitable.

Mills and horses show that the European farmer was doing well. Even more important they show that he was investing in equipment that would increase his output still more. He was ploughing back his profits. This is the key to economic growth. Life in Dark Age Europe was still nasty, brutal and short but now a society existed that was capable of slow improvement.

History is full of surprises. Impressive empires are often socially stagnant and important things happen silently in out-of-the-way places – the improvement of the sailing-ship by the Norse, for example. Though people talk a great deal about our heritage from classical times our present world-wide industrial society has its real roots in Dark Age Europe.

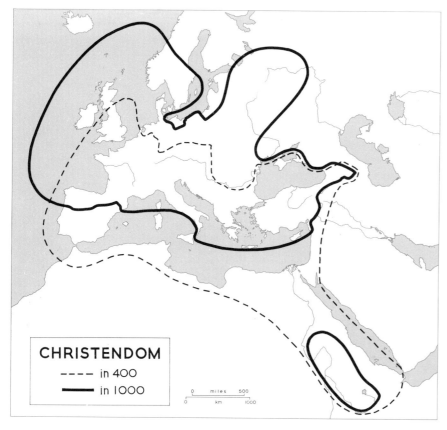

CHRISTENDOM

---- in 400
—— in 1000

miles 500
km 1000

64 THE MONASTERY OF CLUNY IN 1050

In 909 the Duke of Aquitaine gave his hunting lodge at Cluny to a Burgundian abbot for use as a monastery. A few monks moved in and built a little church of the usual basilica type.

The monastery prospered and its efficiency was soon held up as a model to others. Its abbots took over and reformed monasteries all over Europe. This made Cluny famous – and fame brought money from kings and commoners. In 955 work was started on a new church referred to nowadays as Cluny II. It was a much grander structure than Cluny I, nearly twice as long, but structurally a building of the same class. It was finished in 981 but as the money kept coming in, the monks decided on a really daring innovation: they would take off the wooden roof and vault the church with stone.

They knew the Romans had done this with their best buildings and by buttressing the walls they hoped to make them capable of bearing the great weight of a stone barrel vault. They succeeded. The new roof was completed in the year 1000. At last Europe had something that could be called architecture again.

Cluny II was only part of a plan for rebuilding the whole complex. The illustration shows the monastery as it looked when this programme was finished nearly fifty years later.

Immediately over the monastery wall are (from left to right) the hospital, the cemetery and the east end of Cluny II. To the right of the east end of Cluny II a squat tower marks the east end of Cluny I. Beyond Cluny I, in the right-hand corner of the compound, is a guest house. Follow the compound round anti-clockwise – the two-storey building on the far side contains stables and, in the upper storey, a dormitory for the lay brothers. The far corner is occupied by a gatehouse, then there is a dormitory for the junior monks and finally a bath-house which bring us back to the hospital. The big plain building that runs between the bath-house and Cluny II is where the senior monks worked (on the ground floor) and slept (on the upper floor). What we are left with now is the rectangular area between Cluny II and the senior and junior monks' quarters. This area is divided into two cloisters (courtyards) by a dining hall; the far sides of these two cloisters are closed by a bakery (on the left) and a storehouse (on the right). The monastery had about 100 monks and 100 lay brothers (farm-hands and servants). Visitors were encouraged and there was space for over 150.

In the year 1000 Cluny was unique in Europe. By 1100 buildings of the same scale and sophistication were commonplace. This is a measure of the monastery's importance at this turning-point in history. And the role of the monks of Cluny in Europe's medieval awakening was far from over in 1100: by then they were well on the way to completing Cluny III, double the size of Cluny II and the largest church in Christendom.

Sources and Notes

Title For the walls of Constantinople see Van Millingen, A., 'Byzantine
page Constantinople' 1899.

p. 5 The horse-archer is from a fresco in a tomb at T'ung-kou, Manchuria. It is believed to date from the 5th or 6th century. The foot and stirrup have been restored from another example. Stirrups were in use at the eastern end of the steppe in the 5th century but did not reach the western end until the 8th.

p. 11 The plan of Ravenna is diagrammatic: the original Roman grid was certainly distorted to some extent, the southwest gate being 30 m off centre. The names of the churches are the modern ones: some of them originally had different dedications. The 'Palace of the Exarchs' listed in the guide books is the façade of S. Salvatore (14), Theodoric's court church.

The whole of the Ravenna area has dried out since the 6th century. In the town the canals have been filled in and built over and the atmosphere of a little Venice which it must have had in medieval times has completely gone.

p. 15 For the Serpent Column see Volume 1 in this series pp. 47 and 62n.

p. 18 The names of the Roman churches are the modern ones. Many of the dedications have changed over the centuries – in particular St. John-in-Lateran which was originally S. Salvatoris.

p. 20 The inscription commemorates an Arab who died in Fustat ten years after the conquest of Egypt. For the complete text see the Journal of the Royal Asiatic Society, 1930, p. 321

p. 22 The horse-archer is from a painting on a floor in the palace of Qasr al-Hair al-Gharbi (map 24, no. 2).

p. 26 The present mosque of Kairouan dates mainly from a rebuilding by the 3rd Aghlabid Emir of Tunisia in 836, but the arcades round the courtyard are considerably later.

p. 29 The distribution of the T'ang armies is taken from Pullyblank, E.G., 'The Background of the rebellion of An Lu-shan'. OUP 1955.

The lecture hall at Horyuji was originally further forward, the line of the far side of the court at that time being given by the first bend in the sides. Following a fire in 925 a new lecture hall was built on the present site and the verandah carried back to it via the library and belltower. These two buildings had previously stood free behind the courtyard.

p. 30 The cavalryman is one of a series in a fresco of the retinue of the war lord Chang I-chao, a local noble who liberated the Tun-huang area from the Tibetans in 848 and was recognized by the T'ang court as military commander of the region in 851.

It is not strictly true to say that An Lu-shan was a Turk: his mother was a Turk, his father a Sogdian. The Sogdians, the oasis-dwellers of Transoxiana and the Takla Makan, were an Iranian people like the Kushans.

p. 31 The canal system shown on the map is taken from Twitchett, D.C. 'Financial Administration under the T'ang Dynasty'. CUP 1963.

p. 32 The dynasty Clovis founded is called Merovingian after the Frankish
–4 sea-god Meroveus whom Clovis claimed as an ancestor. Charlemagne's dynasty is called Carolingian (after him, Carolus being the Latin for Charles).

p. 34 The two archbishoprics of England have an interesting story behind them. Unlike most of the Germans who moved into the Roman Empire the Anglo-Saxons were not Christian and Pope Gregory the Great had to send a special mission to convert them. His plan called for the setting up of archbishoprics at London and York which had been the capitals of the Roman provinces of lower and upper Britain.

Unfortunately London (the capital of Middlesex) was for a long time resolutely pagan so the southern archbishopric had to be sited in the more friendly kingdom of Kent (capital Canterbury). And King Offa was strong enough to insist on Lichfield, near the Mercian capital of Tamworth, being the seat of the second archbishopric. After Offa's death the northern archbishopric was transferred to York but the Archbishop of Canterbury has never made the move to London.

p. 36 The warriors are from the Franks Casket, which was probably carved in Northumbria c. 700.

p. 37 The Nydam ship is believed to date from c. 250, a century before the beginning of the migration period. A very similar, but much less well-preserved ship was found at Sutton Hoo, Essex, in 1939. It dates from the 6th century and shows that there had been no significant changes in design in the interim.

The terms starboard and port have their origins in the use of a single steering-oar: the ships docked with the steering-oar side (steer-board) away from the port.

p. 39 Like the Oseberg ship the Gokstad ship was found in a burial mound in Vestfold, Norway (in 1880).

p. 42 There are no grapes in Newfoundland but then the Greenlanders can only have had a hazy idea of what grapes were like. Their 'grapes' were probably some sort of berry.

Recently remains of a short-lived iron-using settlement have been discovered at L'anse aux Meadow in the north of the island. If the provisional date of 1000 is confirmed the argument about where exactly Vinland was will be over: no Amerindians could work iron.

p. 46 Neither Mohammed nor the early Caliphs had anything against pictures but by Abbasid times Moslem theologians had come out strongly against any representation of men or animals. This coin of al-Muktadir is one of the rare examples of the prohibition being ignored.

p. 49 If you compare map A with the map of the provinces of the later Roman Empire in Vol. 2 of this series you will see that some of them have been re-arranged in the interim. The changes are all due to Justinian: he combined Honorias with Paphlagonia and Pontus Polemonaiacus with the Armenias and then made a new division of the Armenian area. He also created a little province of Theodoras (T on the map) in honour of his wife Theodora. It consisted of little more than the city of Laodicea-on-Sea and its surrounding territory.

p. 50 Kansu, the province at the Chinese end of the Silk Route, is named after its two major towns, Kan and Su. On map B you will see two other Chinese provinces that have names made up in this way: Ts'in-feng next to Kansu, and Fukien on the coast. Other provinces are named simply after their most important town. In these the town is indicated but not named. The most common type of province name is North (or South or East or West) of X, where X is either the Yellow River (Ho), the Huai River, the Yangtze Kiang, the Tung-t'ing Lake (Hu) or the capital city of K'ai-feng (King). Using the Chinese compass points on map B you can work these out for yourself.

Several provinces have been sub-divided. For example, King-tung (east of King) has been divided into King-tung-si (east of King, western half) and King-tung-tung (east of King, eastern half). In these instances we have translated the third word.

The two provinces furthest south took their name from the capital town of Kuang. After their division Kuang became Kuang-tung which we now know as Canton. Liang-che means the two Che's, i.e. the area to the west of the Che river and the area to the east as well. Yung-hsing chun means 'the province of Everlasting Prosperity'.

p. 51 The concertina-style book is another Diamond Sutra: it was printed in Japan in 1157.

p. 61 The painting of Cluny is by Brian Young. It is based on the reconstruction proposed by the excavator of the complex, Professor K.J. Conant. See Speculum 29, 1954, p. 1.

Index

This is a geographical index to the peoples and places appearing on the maps. It has no entries for the text, photographs, captions or diagrams. As the function of the index is to locate there is only one entry per name. The name is followed by a page number and then by a letter-number combination which gives a reference point inside the map on that page. Entries in capitals have a map to themselves.

Many Chinese towns have changed their names too often for full cross-referencing. For example, the main city of the district of Yen, originally called Yu, has had at least a dozen names in the course of its history. Some of these are combinations of Yen or Yu with -chou and -king, (meaning 'provincial' and 'national' capital respectively). Some of them, like Ta-tu, Khanbalik and Shun-t'ien-fu, are of quite different derivation. The current name is Peking (Pei-king), meaning northern capital. To add to the confusion there are often several ways of writing a Chinese name in our alphabet: the k of king, for example, can be k, ch or p.

Abbreviations:
class. = classical
mod. = modern
syn. = the same as
Byz. theme = Byzantine theme
L. = Lake
R. = River

Acknowledgements for Photographs

Aerofilms 61, 62
Amsterdam, Koninklijk Instituut voor de Tropen 30
Berlin, Staatliche Museum 33
Bern, Bernisches Historisches Museum 16
Broadbent, Simon 21
British Museum, London 3, 4, 35, 50, 54, 55, 56, 58
Clayton, Peter 17, 18
Copenhagen, Nationalmuseet 44
Deutsches Archaologisches Institut, Rome 6
Florence, Biblioteca Medicea-Laurenziana 63
Giraudon 59
Groth, Irmgard 48
Halle/Saale, Landesmuseum fur Vorgeschichte 32
Halliday, Sonia 13
Harvard University, Peabody Museum 46
Hirmer Fotoarchiv, München 8, 9, 14, 51

Japan Information Centre 29
Lane, Emily 10
Limon, José 49
Mansell Collection 5, 7, 11
Mas 1
Office du Livre (photo H. Stierlin, Geneva) 47
Oslo, Universitetets Oldsaksamling 40 and cover
Paris, Bibliotheque Nationale 34
Penguin Books 28 (from Paine and Soper, *The Art and Architecture of Japan*),
  60 (from Rowland, *The Art and Architecture of India*)
Pelliot, Paul 15 (after pl. CCLII in *Les Grottes de Touen-houang*), 31 (after pl. XLIV)
Powell, Josephine 52
Schleswig-Holsteinisches Landesmuseum fur Vor- und Fruhgeschichte 36
Stockholm, Statens Historiska Museum 38, 42, 45
Wood, Roger 26, 27
Younghwan, Huh 57